These chicks know what they are talking about! Having worked closely with both Natasa and Donna I have seen first-hand how they make the impossible possible with their knowledge, experience and energy. They have a knack for promoting businesses and more importantly helping business owners become indestructible in their confidence.
– Juanita Carrington, Boost Groups

Armed with everything you need, Natasa and Donna graciously share all they have learnt in the 10 years of running a home business. For the non-techie it's a must to bring you into the future and for anyone else who is ready to accelerate their business. Take Action – read it and do it Now!
– Kathryn Gregory, Ultimate Mind And Body

The Ninja Business Chicks Business Explosion was very timely for me. Everything that I was hoping for was delivered and it was a practical model to quickly become modern and tech savvy in my business. I would have no hesitation to recommend The Ninja Business Chicks.
– Uncle Steve, Talking Oils

The Ninja Business Chicks are a dynamic duo that has provided an envious amount of information in their Business Explosion workshop. They shared hot tips and resources available to get started with an online presence on a shoe-string budget. Thank you for opening up a new world for my business.
– Mavis Hicks, Aim To Soar

The Ninja Business Chicks, *Natasa Denman and Donna Brown, provided an outstanding training with their Ninja Business Chicks Business Explosion Weekend which filled all of my expectations. I really recommend them if you want to take your business to the next level.*
– Gaby Company, Be Just Yourself

The training offered by The Ninja Business Chicks was an eye-opener and certainly mind-blowing. It doesn't matter what sort of business you are in, it's the process that creates clarity and understanding on how to move forward successfully. Brilliant tools, brilliant delivery and a brilliant change of life!
– Anthony Kilner, Bridging Realms

Thank you Ninja Business Chicks for an inspirational weekend. The way in which the content is presented is extremely user friendly and the tools are excellent and very relevant for growing my business.
– Robyn Ballard, New business starter

Just wanted to say a huge thanks to Natasa and Donna, The Ninja Business Chicks. You are both such inspirations and have given me all the tools and steps to elevate my business to the next step. Watch this space!
 – Vanessa Thomas, Graphic Design Synkd

Ninja Business Chicks are really dynamic and proactive and their mission is to help your home business explode – in a good way! You can get the most from your business with Ninja Business Chicks by attending workshops, training programs, seminars, listening to their podcasts, reading their books and everything else they can think of to make your business soar. They want success for YOU.
– Rosie Shilo, Virtually Yours

Ninja Couch

Marketing

Ninja Couch Marketing

Natasa Denman & Donna Brown

The Ninja Business Chicks (Natasa and Donna) would like to dedicate this book to their hubbies (Stuart and Pickles) for all of their support, encouragement and patience as they work furiously on their businesses with the hope that they can help so many achieve the work life balance they enjoy every day!

Love Red Ninja and Purple Ninja
xxoo

Copyright © 2013 Natasa Denman & Donna Brown

ISBN 978 0 9873597 3 5

Authors: Natasa Denman & Donna Brown
Layout: Blaise van Hecke
Editors: Blaise van Hecke

Typeset in Palatino 11.5/18

Printed and bound in Australia

National Library of Australia Cataloguing-in-Publication entry

Authors: Denman, Natasa, & Brown, Donna

Title: Ninja couch marketing

ISBN: 9780987359735 (paperback)

Subjects: Marketing.

Dewey Number: 658.8

Busybird Publishing
PO Box 855, Eltham, Victoria
Australia 3095
www.busybird.com.au

Contents

Introduction

Welcome to Ninja Couch Marketing!

We are the Ninja Business Chicks. Natasa Denman is the Red Ninja and Donna Brown is the Purple Ninja. We're very excited to be bringing this book to you.

Why are we writing this book? Well, we wanted to share with you our secrets on how we've been able to grow our home-based businesses. We have collectively ten years of experience working from home. Ninety percent of our business is virtual. What that means is we can work from anywhere in the world and generate amazing income for our families.

We wanted to bring and share with you all the tips, strategies and tools that we have used since Day One so that you too can market from the couch. It's really exciting and easy to do when you have the right tools in hand.

So what are the benefits and why would you want to market from the couch? Well it's to save some time, money and to enable you to work from anywhere in the world. This means you can also expand your business internationally. We love to think that we could work from anywhere and enjoy wonderful holidays with our families. And you can end up being the go-to person for solving the problem that needs to be solved. It really grows your credibility and expertise at an international scale.

If you're a home-based business, then this book is definitely for you. However, even if you have a business that's a shop front or you're part of a big corporation, some of the tips and tools in this book will also enable you to do some Ninja Couch Marketing.

So just who are Nat and Donna?

Donna started her business as a virtual assistant, which is like an offsite secretary, seven years ago. She grew that into a successful six-figure practice with a team of virtual assistants working for her. She has various brands that she operates under, some of them being The Office Buddy, The Virtual Assistant Buddy, and she also works closely with the Australian Virtual Business Network.

Natasa started her business in 2010, so two years and eight months ago. She started out as a life coach. However, she soon found out that life coaching does not sell and she niched into weight-loss coaching. She became The Ultimate Weight Loss Coach and launched her brand, Ultimate Weight Loss. She wrote a book, *The 7 Ultimate Secrets to Weight Loss*, and subsequently launched a second brand, Ultimate Business Edge, where she teaches people how to create products for profit.

And now Donna and Natasa have come together as the Ninja Business Chicks because their collective wealth of experience is here to give you the tools so that you can actually create a virtual business that you can run from anywhere in the world.

In this book, you will learn about a variety of different topics. We will start off with Marketing 101, which are the essentials for business success. Then we'll look at how you can step inside your customer's mind. We'll then discuss some goal-setting for marketing success, how to set your goals and achieve all your marketing goals as well as your profit.

It is then we'll get into the juicy stuff. The social media side of your business. It's about how to market yourself in social media, which actually doesn't cost any money at all. We'll look at appreciation marketing and what the hidden secrets of the best entrepreneurs out there are. Then we're going to discuss the awesome power of webinars, forums, YouTube, blogs, how to leverage your content, how to use different tools and resources, and then help you create your ninja plan of attack.

The key to your success is consistency and patience over a long period of time. It isn't a super long process that will take ten years. However, twelve, eighteen months could be the amount of time that you may need to accumulate a following, to be recognized as a credible expert in your field and for people to start coming to you and really approaching you for solutions that you provide through your business.

The sad thing is that ninety percent of you won't even go out and get past the first chapter or even take action on the things we teach. If you choose otherwise, you will reap the rewards from Ninja Couch Marketing. One of our favorite sayings is, "It won't be easy, but it will be worth it."

So enjoy. Sit back. Take all the learning's and put them into action. What we'd like to teach you is that you read each chapter and then take some action following it. It's in the doing that the being comes.

So do the do, and you will have and be the person you want to be as a business owner, and fully successful at marketing from the couch – Ninja Style!

Chapter 1

Marketing 101:
The Essentials of Business Success

Why marketing?

So many people start out in business and fail to realize the importance of marketing. One of the biggest things you can invest your time and education in if you are in business is to invest in your education around marketing.

Collectively, the Ninja Business Chicks have read over 100 books on this particular topic. As a result of reading these books we have gone out there and implemented many different strategies. And we have discovered one sure fact: nine out of ten things that you try around the marketing of your business won't work.

When you do find things that work, guess what you've got to do? You've got to do it over and over and over again. Marketing is absolutely essential for a business to invest in. If they don't have cash flow, they need to spend time to create brand awareness and raise credibility and expertise.

So why would you want to market? Well, the benefit of marketing is brand exposure. Developing trust and relationships with potential clients is critical to any businesses success. Think of it as an explanation of what products and services you provide. It makes it easier for people to refer to you if they understand what brand and what product you actually have. And it also gives the company lots of goodwill.

Put it this way: There is no way that you cannot market. Everything we do, even on a daily basis when we're meeting people out on the street or they've come to a workshop that we have run, everything we do is marketing.

Always remember this from the moment you step outside the house. Even if you're an individual, you are marketing yourself as a certain type of person. So think about marketing as the way you present yourself, the way your brand is presented. If you want people to think you are worth millions, dress like you are worth millions.

What is the perception of your brand out there in the marketplace? Is it aligned with your values, your beliefs and what you want to stand for?

The Ninja Business Chicks have grown to love marketing. We have such passion in doing things and trialing things and measuring to see how is it that we can leverage our expertise, our knowledge, our products, our services in the best way possible so that we can get the highest return and actually work smarter, not harder.

That's something that didn't come easily at the start. We had beliefs that you have to work hard to make lots of money. Until with persistence, consistency and commitment, we came to a realisation that actually there is a way to work smarter, not harder. We have discovered this, and that is why we want to write this book. So we can share that and give you the shortcuts so you don't have to waste as much time as we have.

We're not upset that it's taken us this long to get to where we are. It's a journey. And you need to remember that. When you get in business, you don't need to get to someone else's goal. We believe that there's no goal to be reached. There's always just another level and another level and another level, and we slowly head toward that business mastery.

You are going to get to a point where you say, "I feel like I have arrived." However, that may not be enough. You will find, in the early stages, it may be about money. It may be about you looking after core. It might be looking after the fact that you need to pay the bills and you need to put food on the table.

However, once that's taken care of, life in business becomes more than that. It becomes about helping others be successful. When we help others be successful, our own success gets taken care of.

Another thing that we want to share with you is that it's not just about the marketing that you put out there, but it's also that mindset that you have as a business individual. What is the mindset that you have around your business and the people that are around you? Do you have a growth mindset, or do you have a fixed mindset? Do you have an abundance mindset, or do you have a scarcity mindset? There's quite a big difference there.

And without having to tell you, the abundance mindset and growth mindset are the two that you absolutely need to have to be successful in business. Remember, there is always enough for everyone out there. Just because there are hundreds and thousands of life coaches and even the same amount of virtual assistants, which are the two areas that both Donna and Nat came from, what made a difference is that they believed that they were unique within their field.

This is what you also need to believe. You need to believe that you are the only person that can provide the service or the product and the type of experience for your customer in a unique way, because you are a unique person and there's only one of you in this world.

There are two types of marketing. One is offline, which is the face-to-face stuff. And then there is online, or couch marketing. That is exactly what we will be covering in this book, the "How" of Couch Marketing.

Let's get into the two in a little bit more detail so we can explain what the difference is and how you can go about doing both.

Offline marketing is when you meet someone, you tell them about your business. Perhaps you put up some posters or fliers and they get the person direct mail. You go out networking and you speak to people about your business. That's all offline marketing.

Online marketing is what you do online. It's through your website. It's through social media. It's through different forums such as blogs and YouTube. It could be articles you have submitted to certain websites, which give you exposure and what we like to call back links to your website, so you increase the traffic. There is Google AdWords and social media ads that you can have put up. Those are the variety of things that you can do online.

Now there are things that work online and that don't work online. We like to share the tools and resources that we have used successfully. After all, we didn't have success online from Day One. We persistently studied it. We also read books just like this one to learn how to improve and how to be better at online marketing.

It's all about expanding your focus and finding education so that you can then have the success yourself. Everything you need to know is already out there. There is no need to reinvent the wheel. There is so much information out there these days. You just have to want to find out what it is. So remember, as long as you have a passion for learning and growth, just going back and remembering that growth mindset, that is exactly what you need, and your success will truly follow.

After all, what you focus on is what you get to the exclusion of everything else.

Starting Out

Everybody has to start somewhere. You need to open a Facebook account and depending on your business perhaps a YouTube channel. You need to organise your branding for your business and your logo. It is advisable to set at least a basic website if like most new startups you cannot afford a flashy expensive one. Remember, you do have to start out somewhere.

The most basic things that you need to set up for your business are:

- Your business name
- Your logo
- Your business cards
- Website
- Facebook fan page

These are the five key things that you will need to launch a brand. When you have those, you can really go out there and tell people what problem you solve and start growing your credibility and expertise in that area.

So how do you do this? The answer is through learning. If you already have done a lot of hours work in the particular problem that you solve, you most likely have a lot of experience and knowledge that you can share with people who really are looking for something like you offer.

So remember, there's always someone out there looking for something that you have to offer. Otherwise you wouldn't have a business. It's about being smart and marketing that unique proposition so people see it as a valuable investment to put their money forward.

If you haven't got a niche, it would be very wise to invest some time in working out what you like to do. Figure out what are you good at? What do you like doing? And see if you can turn that into a sellable product or service. After all, if you're going to do it as a business, you want to enjoy what you're doing.

We love training people. We love teaching people all the tips, tricks and tools that we have discovered to get us to the success that we have achieved so far. And it's just so rewarding to see people grow and then report back on their own successes. Just to be that integral part in their success is amazing.

If you're just starting out in business, get yourself set up on Facebook as soon as possible. Open up a LinkedIn account, set it all up and start connecting with the many different people who are online. It's all about building relationships. We will discuss this in the chapters to follow.

Being in business should be fun. It's about creating the life that you desire. You take control and are in charge. You're no longer an employee, you're a business owner. Being a business owner is a choice. Change is by choice, not by chance. And if you feel in the very first months or even the first twelve months, which are the toughest when you are new in business, always remember: every beginning is hard before it becomes easy.

It will become easier. It will become more fun. We remember our first year in our businesses and the doubts that were in our minds. We were saying to ourselves, 'We're not passionate about this. This is not fun.' It was because the amount of effort that we were putting into our businesses was so much compared to the revenue that we were generating.

Natasa generated $7,000 in her first twelve months in business. In her second year, she generated $41,000. In her third year, she cracked through the six-figure income. Getting into her fourth year now, it may even be a seven-figure income.

So everything is gradual. Remember, there's no quick fix. There's no magic bullet. As much as people love to buy that and invest in that, they invest in an easy, quick, fast solution.

You see those ads: lose seven kilos in seven days. Really? Is it really possible? I don't think so. It's all a gimmick. It's all actually marketing.

So how is it that you can market yourself? So when you're thinking about marketing, the one thing to always remember through your product or service that you provide: how is it that your product can ooze easy, simple, fast, step-by-step? How can you create a system that people will invest in? That is the number one key to marketing.

The key is to sell them what they want and give them what they need. People want easy, quick, fast, simple, step-by-step, and hopefully that says that it's some type of a system. It looks nice and formatted and tight.

What do they need? They need all the information, just like you are about to read through twelve chapters in this book that will give you so many tools and strategies. But at the end of the day, if you don't implement them, you're not going to have the results that you want.

This is all about building brand new habits. If so far you haven't been couch marketing, you will need to build that brand new muscle. And to build that brand new muscle or any habit to change for a life, it takes two to three years to build a new neural pathway, or 1,000 times of repetition. Now you're probably thinking, 'Wow! That's a long time!' And that's exactly where we come back to mentioning there is no magic fix. You do have to do the hard work.

Speak to any successful entrepreneur out there and you will find out that they work their butts off. They love what they do. They're passionate about what they're doing. However, do they work hard? Do they work long hours? You betcha!

Creating a Marketing Plan

A marketing plan is a very important tool that you need to make as part of your business.

Month to month and perhaps at the start of the year, you need to plan out what you will do for the rest of the year. It's something that you can be held accountable to. It's a form of setting a goal. And we will discuss that in the goal-setting chapter and how you can go about creating a plan.

It's essential that you do, though. This way you can hold yourself accountable in terms of: are you doing enough marketing week to week, month to month, and what are the measurements for what marketing you've put out there?

We have tried fifty to seventy different ways of marketing our business. How many have been successful? We would say only a handful. Only about four or five different strategies have actually worked.

Natasa's most successful marketing strategies have been networking, running workshops, social media and running some webinars. They are the things that she has done to move her business forward. Prior to that, she tried letterbox drops, newsletters, writing lots of articles to increase the traffic to the website, submitting articles to magazines; all sorts of different marketing strategies, even including Yellow pages and different directories.

However, those were not successful. So what did she do? She doesn't do them anymore. She does the top four that she has had success in, and does them over and over and over again.

The best thing about it is once you learn the things that work, it's really great because every time you do them you know you'll have a return on your investment. And sometimes these things do not have to cost lots of money. We wanted to write this book to give you the tools and the strategies that cost you no money or are very low cost investments when it comes to your marketing dollar. We want you to leverage your marketing dollar in smart ways and not expensive ways.

Marketing is an art. It's an art that you need to keep refining and improving and growing as you grow throughout your business. Early on in business, you will need to use strategies that don't cost a lot of money and you can leverage them as much as possible.

Later on when cash flow is less of an issue, you would probably consider investing in some paid advertising, perhaps through Google AdWords or Facebook advertising. However, in early days, it is very smart to learn the ways that you can leverage your marketing dollar and make it go as far as possible.

So how do you do this? You really need to be able to step inside of your customer's mind. And that is what we'll uncover in Chapter 2 of this book. We need to teach you before you start at marketing about who your customer is. Who is that ideal client? Who is your marketing designed to attract and how do you attract this person into your business?

After all, you cannot be everything to everyone. So many business owners make the mistake of being too generalist. However, as the Americans say, the riches are in the niches, so you do have to have a niche. The best niches are narrow, but deep. If you can find that niche that's narrow, but deep, you will have success that is insurmountable. Remember that. Don't be everything to everyone. Be specific. Be to the point and be a specialist. After all, who earns more money? Is it the GP or the specialist? I think you know the answer to that question.

So strap in. Here we go. We're about to step inside your customer's mind.

Chapter 2

Stepping Inside Your Customer's Mind

In the previous chapter we talked about how your business being everything to everyone is a recipe for disaster. The temptation is always there to say that you're able to solve the problem of many varied people or businesses.

For example, a hairdresser that says I'm looking for anyone with hair is always too broad. Saying I specialise in helping women around the age of thirty to fifty that have dry and frizzy hair to have it looking silky and smooth, now that's being very specific. I certainly know many women out there who are sick of their frizz and belong to this category.

For example, if you're one of those women who have never found a solution for frizzy hair, are you more likely to go to a generalist hairdresser or one that specialises in solving that particular problem?

As I said also in the previous chapter, the most successful strategy is to work in a niche that is narrow, but deep. What that means is that the more specific you are around the exact problem that you solve, the higher sales and success rate you will have as a result.

Also, you can charge a lot more. After all, as we said, who earns more money? The GP, or the specialist doctor? A deep niche means that there are plenty of people or businesses out there with that exact problem that will pay to have it solved.

So getting inside your customer's mind is about you also deciding your positioning and presence in the market. How do you want to be perceived, and who is this ideal client? So what we would like you to do is actually go through and answer as much as possible writing out the answers to the list of questions that we give you.

Here are the questions:

- Your ideal client title.

- What is their name? You need to choose a name for your ideal client. Because when you're writing your marketing copy, you want to have this person in mind. You almost actually want to design this person. You want to give them a name.

- What age are they?

- Where do they live?

- Do they have a family?

All of those bits and pieces have to be answered because when you are planning your marketing, you are writing to this particular person. You want to be able to write to one person only when you're writing your marketing.

Here is another load of questions that we would love you to answer.

- What do they want?

- What are their secret desires?

- What keeps them awake at night?
- How do they want to be seen?
- Who are they really behind closed doors?
- What motivates them?
- What is the attitude of my ideal client?
- How much money are they making and why?
- What is their purpose in life?
- How do they communicate in their world internally and externally?
- What does my ideal client value?
- What keeps them going when the going gets tough?
- If they were to achieve everything they want, what would they wish they had?
- What do they believe to be true about the world?
- What do they believe about their current situation?
- What do they believe their current situation means to them?
- What will their ideal situation mean to them?
- How does my ideal client language their world?
- How would they describe themselves?
- Do they have multiple streams of income?
- Do they have limiting beliefs? Are they making a difference? And if so, why?
- Do they like learning?
- What role do they play in the business?

- Is it about getting up every day and going to work for someone else?

- What type of people do they hang out with?

- What are their interests and hobbies?

- Do they like to stretch themselves out of their comfort zone?

- What inspires them?

- Do they wish they had more time?

- What type of life are they living? In a rut, or the one that they imagined?

- What do they need to improve or change to step up?

Once you have answered these questions in a lot of depth and detail, you will become very familiar with whom your ideal client is.

What we found in our businesses is that we started noticing that we were attracting certain people. And these people had certain characteristics, and we would know when we met our ideal client. They would have answers to these questions that we just posed that matched what we had given answers to.

As you get on in business, you get to know your ideal client quite intimately and you know what makes them tick. An easy way to complete this exercise is to give it a go, first by yourself, and then, if you can, actually incentivize some of your clients to go through and answer it for you, especially the ones who are really happy with your services. Why is it that they came to you? What problem did they have? And how did you go about solving that problem? That will give you more credibility and it will increase the power of your marketing, because you're not the only person who's come up with the answers. It's actually the people who have used your products and services that have given you assistance in these answers.

A suggestion would be to give them a gift or give them some kind of a discount off their next purchase. Something like that so that you can get into their heads. What Natasa did in her weight-loss business was to answer questions for her ideal client and then she got a few people who were friends, perhaps that were struggling with their weight, to also help her out and get some of the answers. That's how she structured her marketing when it came to the ideal client for that particular business.

Another thing that is very important for your clients is who you represent. Because at the end of the day, your client is actually not so much buying your product and service, but they're buying you. So you need to represent who they want to become. A hairdresser with messy hair? I don't want to go to someone like that.

When Natasa started out in her weight-loss business, she couldn't have been successful had she been overweight. She had to stand and look and act like her ideal client – who they wanted to become. That is what made the difference. Nowadays, Natasa has also licensed her Ultimate Weight Loss business and she's got other weight loss coaches using her business-in-a-box setup. And it is critical that those coaches have to look the part. Otherwise, she knows that they will not attract clients and be able to convert them into paying clients, because they don't look like the person that their client wants to become.

We couldn't have been the Ninja Business Chicks had we

not had success in our businesses. Had we not grown our credibility and expertise in these areas so that we can now teach others what we had then. If we didn't do at least six figures in our businesses, we wouldn't be sitting here talking to you. It just wouldn't be right. We're only talking to you so that we can show you the way you can model what we have done so that you can re-create it in your life.

After all, the fastest way to success is when you model someone who's been there before and you actually avoid the things that don't work and do the things that this particular model has done that have worked.

Had we had our second go at doing our businesses, of course we would do it a lot faster. After all, we have learned from the feedback we received in the earlier days in business. We don't regret having taken seven years for Donna, two-and-a-half to three years for Natasa. We don't regret any of that because we know it's a journey. Everyone does it at a different speed.

So please, don't compare yourself to anybody else out there. This is your own individual journey. You have different circumstances to other people. Perhaps you are a parent. Perhaps you're looking after someone with disability. Or perhaps you're single and free and you have time abundance where you can invest as much time and energy and really skyrocket your business in a speedy time frame.

This is a mistake that Natasa made in her business early on when she was comparing herself to other people who had gotten the paying clients. She didn't get a paying client for the first five months and thought that this wasn't the speed that she usually would do things at. She considered herself a high achiever. Not having had a paying client for five months was something that was not part of what she stood for and she thought she would be able to achieve her success a lot faster.

Nowadays both the Ninja Chicks know that everyone's journey is individual, and that is what we're here to teach you. We're here to also teach you that this is a journey of ups and downs, frustrations and celebrations and successes, and some setbacks. And that's OK. Any journey to success is not a straight line. It's actually a really, really messy line that goes back and forward, front and back. You sometimes will end up seeing that you go two steps forward and sometimes a step or two backward. As long as you just push through and know that with your persistence you will find the things that work for you.

Maybe even some of the strategies that we teach you won't specifically work for you, and others will work for you a lot faster than they worked for us. So you will find your own recipe. It's about investing in education, reading through this book and taking the actions.

Once again we'd like to remind you of the standard marketing smarts around what your customer wants. So going back to what we discussed in Chapter 1, sell them what they want and give them what they need.

Every time you put out any marketing copy, whether it's naming your product, running your workshops and naming those, or putting together some packages, what you've got to do is actually pick 'sexy' names.

We like to call them sexy because they really make the customer feel like they want to find out what is going to be in this product? What is going to be in this workshop? And what is going to be in this package? Should I take it up with this business owner?

So what does sexy mean? Well, using hypnotic words in naming your products, packages, your CDs if you record CDs, or even your workshops that you want to invite people to. For example, this particular book has got a sexy name. People are curious, 'What is Ninja Couch Marketing? I really am curious about finding that out.'

Natasa's other book, *The 7 Ultimate Secrets to Weight Loss*, again has got hypnotic language. The word 'ultimate', the word 'secrets'. People love that there are only seven. That's like, 'Oh, I've got to find out what those seven are, and if I do those seven that means I'll lose all my weight!' Will you really? It's actually all marketing smarts in terms of naming the product.

Remember that ninety percent of people will purchase your product, services, workshop and packages, because of the name that you have given them. Sometimes that is all that it takes to get someone interested. Headlines, things like that, are very, very important to be on top of.

What you can do to find out what hypnotic words are that you can use is go to Google and you'll come up with lots of documents that actually will give you hundreds of hypnotic words. Hypnotic words such as amazing, awesome, outstanding, instant, unbelievable, ultimate, sale, free and unlimited are all hypnotic words.

So remember, your customers want something that's going to promise them that it's going to be amazing. That there are only five steps, or seven or whatever number you choose. Is it that there is twelve secrets to achieving whatever solution they're looking for, for their problem?

When you want to step inside your customer's mind, the first is in the way that you name your products and services. That is very, very crucial. The name needs to ooze easy, simple, fast, step-by-step. It's a system.

We like to use numbers, for example when naming our workshops. One such workshop was "The 3 Secrets to Losing All Your Unwanted Weight."

Natasa had a do-it-yourself program that was "7 Hours to Achieving Your Ultimate Body." But can you really achieve your Ultimate Body in seven hours if you're 20 kilos overweight? Possibly not, but it's a play on words. How can you also use that play on words?

Secondly, if you are putting together a manual or book such as this, you also need to use hypnotic words in terms of the outline such as the chapter names. This is because once someone looks at a title, they'll also want to look at what's below that and find out, 'Do I want to continue reading it,' and would they want to buy it. So give your outlines as well something that people want to find out. You want to arouse their curiosity. You want to leave them hanging for the content that you're about to deliver.

For example, look back at this book. The very first chapter was Marketing 101: The Essentials for Business Success. Chapter 2 is Stepping Inside Your Customer's Mind. How do you step inside your customer's mind? Chapter 3 will be about goal-setting for marketing success. The word success is a hypnotic word. So use those types of words throughout your marketing copy. That is what people want.

When they actually come to you, you give them what they

need, which is actually all the steps and the fact that there is no magic bullet. That they will have to work hard to get the solution that they're after to the specific problem.

We will even wrap up this chapter for you. Remember, the takeaway points from this are to work out who you are and what you stand for. How do you want to be perceived as a business and who is that ideal client that you want to appeal to?

Remember that you should not be marketing to everyone. It's a surefire way to disaster.

Remember to do all the exercises and answer all the questions. This way you can really get inside your customer's mind. What do they actually want? How do you actually put out your product and services? How do you name them?

Use the hypnotic language. Sell them what they want. Give them what they need.

Chapter 3
Goal-Setting for Marketing Success

The pinnacle of being a successful business owner is the ability for you to successfully and consistently set your big-vision goals and breaking them right down into smaller goals.

Goals really give you the ability to prioritize and to remove the feeling of being overwhelmed and to do what you have set out to do. They really tap into your subconscious mind, giving it direction for you to achieve what you once thought impossible.

Both the Ninja Business Chicks regularly set their goals. The best goals to set in business are your ninety-day goals, your one-year goals and your bigger, five-year vision.

Goals should be set around your business activities as well as your personal life and your marketing. Marketing goals are very, very important because if there's no marketing for your business, then you will not have a business at all.

What we also like to do is once we have set our shorter-term goals of ninety days, we even break them down into weekly tasks or targets. We break those down into weekly targets so that we can be held accountable to ourselves. We have them right in front of our face.

The Red Ninja, Natasa, likes to use a manual diary where she will write down her goals and tick them off, whereas the Purple Ninja uses her online diary. And that's fine. Whatever suits you and your personality is great, as long as you're using something.

The difference between people who use diaries and journals and those who don't is that the ones using the diaries, do take responsibility and know that they have a choice in creating amazing success in their lives.

If you're not using a diary, what are you avoiding? I would say you are avoiding responsibility and living in a very dependent state, or you have childish behavior. Stephen Covey talks about this in a book called, *The 7 Habits of Highly Effective People*. He says that when you're dependent, you avoid responsibility. You're very childish and you don't want to be using a diary or being tied to something. When you're independent, you are using it. You're acting of your own accord and you're taking responsibility.

And then there's another stage that he talks about. He talks about interdependence. Interdependence is where you actually help others through you. Both Natasa and Donna have been able to reach that interdependent status. We have achieved that through being able to reach out and help business owners like you to achieve success in their businesses. We are already taken care of. We've been independent for a long time. Now it is about us moving forward and helping others achieve their dreams.

Goal-setting is one of the core things and core keys to our success. Why do people not set goals? There's one simple answer: familiarity. Goal-setting gets talked about so much nowadays that people tend to ignore it because they become too familiar and it has become something that they take for granted.

It shouldn't be that way. The power of goal-setting should not be underestimated. It's truly magical. Not only do we set goals, we also have vision boards. We also have affirmations of things and the people who we want to become. But we're not quite there yet.

The Red Ninja, Natasa, has her affirmations laminated on the back of her shower door so while she's having a shower, brushing her teeth, she reads her affirmations. So she kind of is killing three birds with one stone. That's worked really, really well. She never thought this possible when she put those up in her shower in the first six months of starting her business. Now they play such a vital part and are so true in her life.

These were affirmations such as, 'I'm a master in business. I'm a master at sales and marketing. I'm a master at communications and influence. I can work from anywhere in the world. I'm always patient and present to my children and their needs. I'm healthy, strong and vital.'

These are just some examples. You need to make them specific for yourself and to really, really repeat them and read them twice a day. The same thing goes for your goals. A full page of your ninety-day goals, one for your one-year goals, and then a description: what does your life look like in five years' time?

The central thing to remember with goal-setting is to write them in the present tense and as if you are already in possession of them, this is critical. You want to get your unconscious mind to already think that it has arrived there.

What happens with goal-setting is that it creates tension in our brain. We're saying we want to be over there, but we're still over here, and that starts to make us feel uncomfortable. It makes us want to move.

A lot of you in the background might be saying, 'Well I've set goals in the past and they never come true, what's the point?' I hear you and I can give you a couple of examples as to why goals don't come true. Goals don't come true because you're already happy where you're at right now in your life. So then why would you do anything more? Are you already addicted to the way you're feeling?

Some people are so addicted to feeling sad and depressed and sorry for themselves that they don't know any other way of life. They've just built the muscle around feeling in that negative and unresourceful state, and they just can't snap themselves out of it. It's important that if this is you that you start your affirmations today. Write your goals and write your goals in different categories.

The five categories we recommend that you set goals in are:

- Personal development
- Business and career
- Family relationships
- Health and wellness
- Financial materialistic goals

We will give you an example of what a goal might sound like. This is the Red Ninja reading out one of her ninety-day goals. It always starts with the date when the goal is supposed to have been achieved. When we were writing this book it was 2012. This is what she has written.

It's the 31st of March, 2013, and I have a total of 30 licensees on the books. The start of this year has been amazing. We are now taking in $15,000 per month. Stuart (Natasa's husband) and I together have sold $100,000 in licenses, products and trainings. We have also registered for GST. I have three international licensees with more interest coming through regularly. I feel the momentum is gaining more speed. I hear my phone ringing with three inquiries every week and I see twenty new signed licensing contracts.

So you can see in this particular goal, it's written in the present tense as if I'm already in possession of it. By the end of it, I have said what I will feel, hear and see, because that automatically engages all of my modalities of the visual, kinesthetic and auditory, which means I can actually paint a really vibrant picture of what that day looks like. It really is awesome. When I read it, it just fills my heart with happiness and I totally believe that it's possible.

The one thing with your goals, you do have to believe in them. If you don't believe something is possible, you will be right. If you do, you will also be right at the same time as well.

So set the different goals. What we also recommend is that if you are using a manual diary or even an online one, use different colours for different things in your life. We like to use blue for our family engagements, green for our regular appointments or mentoring sessions, let's say, or something that we do on a regular basis. Red is the hot new leads and prospects. Something that we're about to have an amazing sale or an opportunity. Black is for our business commitments and meetings.

You can take those on board and see if the colour coordination works for you if you like. It really helps you learn and remember a lot better. We weren't designed to just learn in black-and-white. Colour is a very powerful way to actually remember things. That is why children are taught to use different colour crayons and pencils so we always use colour.

Your Marketing Plan

Just like goal-setting, the marketing plan should be mapped out.

It's almost like you're setting goals for what marketing you commit yourself to complete over ninety days or one year. If one year is quite a long time for you to map out, then sit down and map out your next three months as you should know what is going to happen in the next ninety days.

Sit down and write out what sort of activities you will do. Will you be attending some networking events? Will you be spending a specific amount of time on social media? Will you write some articles and submit them to publications? Will you go and approach certain businesses to set up some joint ventures? How many coffee chats will you have with people who you come in contact with who possibly may connect you with someone who you could set up a joint venture with? Are you going to run any workshops for your business? After all, that's marketing as well.

So really sit down. In Word, there are calendars. What we used to do is print off a monthly calendar, so for January or February or March. Then we insert all the different activities that will be done depending on where it is in the week. Even include the newsletters that you send to your database as that's also a marketing activity.

All these activities are really good for you to also then log all of your marketing activities on your spreadsheet. We have enclosed in the appendices, a copy of a marketing activities spreadsheet. This is very simple to use and it's something we use every week. Whenever we sit down to write out our weekly reports, which consist of a weekly dashboard where we log income expenses.

The second thing that we do is sit down and log in what kind of marketing activities we had and what was the result of those? This is where the measurement comes in. So when you actually have a look at what your marketing activities have been over an extended period of time and what your outcomes have been, then you get a very clear picture as to what's been successful and what has not been such a good use of your time.

Make this habit. Again, build a muscle. If you do it early enough in your business if you are new, perhaps you won't have so much to put in there. As you grow, more and more will go into these marketing activity spreadsheets, and you can see that it's a lot easier to do. It only takes ten minutes to do both of those reports at the end of a week. Just like big corporations require people to complete reports at the end of each week, treat your business as if it's a big corporation, because if you do that Day One, you will end up being a big company which has amazing systems.

Systems are very important in business, because ultimately they replace you having to sell your time for money. And at the end of the day, going into business for yourself, that is the ultimate outcome. We stop selling our time for money, and that we have people either employed or we end up exiting our business and selling it for an awesome sum that keeps you secure for the rest of your life financially.

Enjoy your business in the meantime. Spend a little bit of time each week, an hour, hour and a half, writing your systems. Both the Red and Purple Ninja, within some of their other brands, did this for an extended period of time. It didn't happen overnight. That's how they were actually able to put all the bits and pieces together so that they can come up with a program, a license, and then sell businesses in a box to other people who could start making money out of it straight away.

Again, at the end of the day you want to end up with a system, because a system is something that can turn into a turnkey business that you can sell time and time again. Just look at the McDonald's model. They were put out there and so many people benefitted. There's so many amazing franchisees who benefit from the McDonald's model.

However, who is the richest person out of it? It's Ray Kroc, the man who started McDonald's.

Remember this. The key is in the systems.

So far in the book, we have discussed Marketing 101 and why it is important, how you can get inside your customer's mind.

Then it was the importance of goal-setting and for you to create the mindset that you need to be a successful business person.

Take some time and actually read books on mindset. Read the book *Think and Grow Rich* by Napoleon Hill. That's an amazing book where he studied about 500 successful business owners and how they thought. And he found common patterns around how successful people think. Invest time in studying this as well.

So first of all I said invest some time in educating yourself around marketing. Secondly, I'm also saying invest your time educating yourself around the mindset of successful people.

The core books that the Ninja Business Chicks read are marketing books, business mindset books, and books that are relevant to the niches that they operate in. Once again, it is not about re-inventing the wheel. It's about finding the recipe that works. After all, whatever you do is going to be unique, because there's only one of you in this world and you are unique.

At the end of this chapter I want to touch on a point around perfection. Perfection doesn't serve you. It doesn't serve anybody. We like to define perfection as looping and insanity because you never get anything finished because it's never good enough.

The important thing is to let go. It's better to have done something at eighty percent than to do nothing at one hundred percent. Let go of the 'stuff' because it makes you human if you actually have mistakes in some of your products or training materials.

Perhaps you found a few mistakes in this book so far. That's okay with us because we're not about perfection. We know that the content we've got within here is going to make a really big difference in your life and your business. We want to get it out there so we can help you. If you find a spelling mistake, it doesn't really matter; this isn't a book about spelling

Is it all that important? Focus on the things that matter, the things that count. Do more of those things. Outsource anything that takes the time away from you doing what you're passionate about and what you're good at. If you're getting paid $200 an hour for what you do, don't go around doing the cleaning at home or the gardening. Hire someone to do that for you and pay them $30 an hour.

In the early days, that might not be possible. However, if you have good financial smarts and you do it at the right time, it will become possible and then you have more time to invest earning higher amounts as well as continuing to grow and help others.

It is about helping others at the end of the day. We're human beings that thrive on contribution and growth.

To wrap up this chapter, here's a couple of tasks for you:
- Go out and set your ninety-day and one-year goals
- Set your five-year vision
- Put together your ninety-day marketing plan

We also advise you to write out your top ten affirmations that have meaning to you. Make them specific. Who do you want to become in the future? Do that even though you may not be that person right now but write it down as it will drive you, so make the changes you need.

Affirmations are also meant to be written down in the present tense, as if you are already in possession of them. They're just little shortcuts to what your ultimate vision is and who you want to be.

Chapter 4
Social Media Gold

One of the most powerful mediums where you can advertise your business at no cost is the social media platforms.

The two strongest ones that have made the biggest difference in our businesses have been Facebook and LinkedIn. If you're not currently set up on these platforms, we suggest that you do it right now. The power of building relationships through social media is unbelievable. That's what it's all about: building relationships.

Building relationships is about growing the trust. Getting people to like you, trust you, and then they buy from you. That is exactly how it happens.

If the intention of building a relationship is just to make a sale, then you haven't got the right intention. The intention should always be to find out how you can help other people. Perhaps contacts you have that you can share? Can you help each other out? Or simply just end up having a social connection that may turn into something else later on.

People ask us should they use their personal Facebook page for business or should they create a fan page? I believe both are really good. One key rule that I love to apply to Facebook and LinkedIn is that I never post anything negative.

No one likes to be around negative people. We all want to feel that there is positivity around us. We like to feel that other people are contributing to our lives rather than taking away from them.

The private Facebook page is more about you giving something away from yourself about your private life. Sharing your successes and upcoming events are two other good things to post. From time to time you can give people updates about your business, but it's more about building relationships. That's what you're doing on your private page.

On your Facebook fan page, the intention is there to add value and really deliver what is the reason why you're in business. Through educating people around the tips and tricks that you have to solve the problem that you do, that is how people get to know you, like you and then ultimately visit your business or contact you to do business with you.

Our recommendation is that you add value. Six or seven posts, and then you can post something that sells something to the public. Make them an offer as there's so many different ways that you can leverage social media. One of the ways is to advertise your events and invite people who you think might be interested in attending. It's a fantastic way to fill the room when it comes to running workshops and webinars. And we will be discussing webinars a bit later on.

Facebook also has paid advertisements. You can put up an

offer and segment it to who actually gets the offer. You can choose that only females age twenty-one to twenty-seven view it. Perhaps from an area that's local. Let's say we're in Melbourne, so we want to target females twenty four to twenty seven who are in Melbourne, Australia. It's an amazing way to spread the message as well as get lots of leads and prospects into your business.

The strategy that the Ninja Business Chicks have used since Day One around their social media has been to build on their contacts. Build friends on Facebook and build on the connections on LinkedIn. When you have a high number of contacts, connections and friends, you have more leverage in terms of when you put out an offer or an event to have people attend it or take it up.

That's why our social media strategy has been to connect with ten people each day on LinkedIn as well as on Facebook. A lot of people go, 'Oh, that's easy. I'll just click, click, click, connect with people, and that'll be fine.' You always want to be connecting with people who have mutual friends with you as well as mutual connections, perhaps on LinkedIn.

When you connect with someone and they accept your request, a professional thing is to actually send them a very casual, informal hello. An example is, 'Hey there. Thanks. It's great to connect. Thanks for accepting my request to connect. I see that you are …' and then you insert their business, 'What are you looking for specifically? I would love to find out more. I'm looking forward to getting to know you better. All the best…' and you can sign out.

We have had entrepreneurs respond to us. Very, very successful people respond to us in such a casual way, even as far as saying "cheers" at the end. Social media is about being really informal. It's not about writing this structured business letter. It's about being friendly and just, 'Hi, how are you doing?'

If the person responds, and not everyone will – you may only have a response rate of one in ten – or if you find a formula that really works and gets your percentage of response rate a lot higher, then keep doing that.

We recently met a person who had a sixty percent response rate to their messages. And we asked him, what was the difference? What did he do that made the difference? And what he said is, 'All I did is I asked people to catch up for coffee, especially if they were local.' What we thought was, 'Oh my God, that's such a good idea. You get straight to the point.' Some people will say yes. Some people will say no. It pays to be more direct and to actually get straight to the point than being just way too general.

When you do get a message back, then perhaps you can elaborate on a little bit about what you do because you're expecting that the person has responded about what they do. Generally if they tell you about what they do, they will also ask you about what you are looking for. This is your opportunity to have a succinct template put together where you let them know how you help people and what you're looking for in your business.

It's a great idea to actually have a few templates drawn up. You can have separate templates for LinkedIn and separate templates for Facebook. Instead of doing them time and time again, it's good to use these templates to cut and paste into the messages so they go out a lot quicker. If you're connecting with ten people every day on each platform, you want to be on top of starting all the conversations.

This has been the most powerful way that we have grown our businesses. We have created them into a business that can be run anywhere in the world. Most successful entrepreneurs do this or they have their virtual assistant help them do it. However, it's coming from their account so that you think that they're contacting you. Then model that.

If you want to have success in your business, you have to model what successful people do. I would say have a minimum of two templates. One is a short intro and one that explains exactly what you do and what you are looking for. Invest time and help people. That is the clear-cut message here. You need to remember that people like to know that you're interested in them and that you're there to help them.

Add value eighty percent of the time and sell twenty percent of the time. So use that 80/20 rule.

Otherwise, you can also increase your social media status and increase the likes on your fan page by participating in groups where you post comments as your fan page, because there are two different ways you can post comments. As you the individual or by you as the fan page. If people like what you're saying and you're adding value to group discussions, they will go back to your fan page, have a look, check it out and perhaps like it.

A fan page becomes really, really profitable for a business owner once it clicks over 1,000 likes. Something that we found out recently was that if you have over 400 likes, you can actually post special little offers that people can claim from your business. They're really handy to have. We've trialed them and people do like and click them and claim the offer.

You're probably wondering, 'Well how powerful can social media be?' One day Natasa the Red Ninja connected with a lady on LinkedIn. She sent her little template intro. This lady then wrote back, and Natasa got back to her straight away again. The lady wrote back again. And within a couple of hours, they had arranged to have a phone conversation two hours later. Within four hours, they were on Skype. They had the conversation, and the lady signed up as a paying client.

The conversion through social media can occur so fast. It doesn't happen every single time. A lot of other times you'll find that you do have to build relationships over a longer period of time. People have to see that you are serious about what you do and that you are that credible expert.

To get a client in five hours without even leaving your house is absolutely amazing. It is the cold calling of the 2000s.

Other times we have done it in a day or two where we've connected and started to meet up with a person, or yet again set up a spot meet or a GoToMeeting type of setup where you meet the person online. It truly is powerful.

LinkedIn also has groups where you can participate and ask questions. And it's really great to be part of groups like this because it gives you exposure, and if you're adding amazing value into the group, you will be seen as this incredible expert that people will want to go to time and time again, and they will look you up.

The whole point is if you're active on social media and people like what you're saying, they will look you up and look up your website. If they're in the market for the solution that you're selling, they'll definitely contact you.

It's something that should not be underestimated and you should be part of it even if you're scared of technology and don't know how to do it.

It's fantastic if you can get your contacts over 1,000 friends on Facebook. Work toward that goal, same as your fan page, 1,000 likes. See if you can get your connections on LinkedIn over 500. If you can get those over 500, you automatically look like a big company, because LinkedIn only counts connections up to 500 and then it says 500+ which is a really magnificent way to look like you're more successful than you potentially are early on in the business.

Make sure that you're always responding to people. If they write a comment or click like or whatever it is, respond back. People like to know that they're being interacted with. That is the whole magic of social media. Back and forward, back and forward, back and forward, just like a normal conversation except it's happening through typing and chatting perhaps through private messages.

Remember to always follow up as well. If someone has requested something from you, you want to follow up. Sometimes someone may say, 'Yes, I would like to buy this product from you,' and you send them a message and then you invoice them and then they don't come back to you. This can happen. What you need to do is perhaps write it into your journal and say, 'In a week's time I'll just touch base with them and see how they're going.'

I can't tell you how many times we have had people go through with a sale even though we originally got in touch with them, then it probably wasn't in the centre of their attention, then got back to them and they finished off the sale, they paid their invoice and they got their product or service that they were requesting.

Follow-up is huge in business, not just through social media. If you're networking you also need to follow up with people. Set up some appointments where you can get to know them. If you go out networking face-to-face, just by attending a networking event, perhaps you don't learn so much about anyone too specifically because you may meet three, four, five people and you don't have the time to get to know exactly what they're after and how to help people. It's really amazing to actually catch up for a coffee chat.

That's why with our social media strategy, the whole intention is actually to end up having that half-an-hour or hour conversation with a person over Skype or GoToMeeting. If you can have that conversation, you can actually get to know each other a lot better. Maybe you're not a fit to work together however, you'll never know that unless you have a conversation with the person at the other end.

Comments and questions and messages are one thing, but the human touch and the human interaction over seeing each other face-to-face, at least over the computer, it's a lot more powerful and you get to hear the person's tone of voice. You get to sense their personality and you actually get to see what they're about.

If they're a client, are they committed? What are their needs? What would they like to achieve through working with you? If they're someone you potentially want to hire, you see them as a professional. How do they look at the other end? How do they represent themselves? What do they seem like? Do you seem like you're a match to work together?

The follow-up process is super, super important. It's something that should be part of daily business activities. You should always, always note down when you need to follow up with people. Don't rely on your memory because it will let you down. There are just so many things in business that we need to keep track of that things can slip from our mind.

Always write it in whenever you have to do a follow-up phone call. That way you keep your mind clear on the things that are important and that you need to be focusing on.

So to wrap up Social Media Gold, the takeaway point out of this is be part of Facebook. Be part of LinkedIn. It's very, very powerful for business. In the bonus chapter you will see there is an interview by a social media expert who actually does that as his business. He helps businesses be very visible and very interactive on all of the social media platforms whichever ones they want to be a part of.

You will read some of the strategies that he will teach us on how to improve your social media presence and how to improve your lead generation for your business. We're very excited to share this amazing knowledge that he has.

But what you want to do is start. Start somewhere, create an account. Create your profile. Keep it simple. Make it attractive. As we said earlier, make it sexy so that people will be curious to find out more. Start interacting with people. Connect with people. You don't have to do it seven days a week. Make it part of your daily activities. Maybe you'll connect with people and spend half an hour each day on social media seeing what's come in, what needs to go out, who you need to respond to and perhaps posting some valuable information on your fan page and on your personal page to share with people.

Start today because it does take time. It takes time and patience to build an amazing business that generates profits from the free marketing of social media.

Chapter 5

Appreciation Marketing:
Hidden Secrets of the Best

The world has moved so fast. Nowadays, we no longer get the postcard in the mail for our birthday. Instead, we get an e-mail message to go click on a link and connect to a page where our birthday wishes are awaiting us.

Things have changed dramatically. However, getting something in the mail is something that is so nice. It still gives you that appreciation of the person that has sent it to you.

Again, we go back to building relationships. The importance of doing this as a business owner is first and foremost. If you cannot build relationships sincerely and honestly, then you won't have a successful business.

Since we started our businesses, we have used postcards or thank you cards as part of an everyday activity that we do in our business. It is part of our systems and systems are something that's very important to have set up when it comes to building relationships. You want to be able to remember a person's birthday or a note to say thank you to them if they've sent a referral your way. You can send out an Easter card and a Christmas card or congratulations if they've achieved a certain goal.

What we have been using is a company called SendOutCards. SendOutCards is an amazing system that you can use right from the couch. After all, this is about couch marketing. It's an online system where you can go in and create a postcard, put in your personalized message, change it whichever way you want. You don't even have to use a template postcard. You can even put a photo on the front and then it gets printed, packaged and posted to your client for as little as $1.50.

You can't even get a card that cheap at the $2 Shop. That's including the postage. It's all automated, which means you can enter all your addresses. Your whole database can be entered. People's birthdays can be entered and the system reminds you ten days or two weeks ahead of their time that it's their birthday and to go in and click and send them a card.

The best thing about this system is that it also allows you to set up campaigns. What are campaigns? Campaigns are cards that you will use over and over again. So for example if you wanted to send a Happy Birthday card, you don't have to change this card every single time for every single person. You can just set up a campaign for the year. You might want to change it over in the next year so they don't get the same card.

You set this campaign up and then you can put in {first name}, which enters everyone's first name depending on who you're sending it to, write your nice message and then sign off.

The same thing goes if someone becomes a client for the first time. Perhaps you want to have a client welcome card. Or if you're a coach or a trainer, perhaps if you've conducted training, at the end of it you've taken a photo of the group, you might want to insert the group photo.

Whenever the Red Ninja did short workshops, any type of training, she used to do this exact thing. Get the whole group together to celebrate the completion of that workshop and training, and then about a week later they would get a card in the mail saying how wonderful it was to have them there, and then they'll have a little memento of the workshop.

Appreciation marketing is not really about selling yourself and putting your branding all over the cards. People know who you are and what you do. It's something more social rather than salesy. In this day and age, marketing is not really about that hard push and hard sell and being really obvious that you're being sold to. It's about building the relationship and being a person of integrity, a person that is there to help out their potential client, and someone who is looking out for you in your time of need. That is what a business owner does nowadays to be a successful business owner. You're filling the gap that exists in that person's life.

With SendOutCards, it's so amazing that you can even scan in your own personal handwriting so it actually looks even more personalized. There is also a handwriting type of font that you can use and that's what we have used. A lot of people think that we actually wrote on this card. That's an amazing way of people going, 'My God, she really took the time to sit down and put these together and send that out to me.'

You get saved a trip to the post office. The cost of sending cards and the quality of cards that are in SendOutCards are top notch. They're the same quality that you get from an $8 John Sands card.

If you are a work from home business owner, most likely you have quite personal relationships with your clients and they're quite one-on-one, let's say. It might not be the case, but a lot of the time it is. That is why appreciation marketing is so important for you to make part of your daily business activities. It reminds you, it prompts you and it keeps you connected and that's the important thing in business, to stay connected. To stay top of mind with your customers.

Another thing I'm going to add into this chapter is the absolute need for you to have a regular newsletter, a newsletter that you also are doing from your couch. If you don't know how to do it yourself, hire someone to design your newsletter template, and then all you have to do is actually put in your content and then click send. And then your client at the other end receives a ready-made newsletter that looks professional. It looks like it's been put together by a big corporation and not someone who is from a home-based business.

Both the Ninjas do these for their clients. The Red Ninja sends out a fortnightly newsletter and that goes out every fortnight without fail. Even if she's away on a holiday, she schedules newsletters to go out on the right time or she just pops them in while she's away, because doing things from the couch allows you to do things also from your holiday couch.

The Purple Ninja does the same. Part of her virtual assistant business does this for other people. If this is not your strength, to write a newsletter for your business, you can always hire virtual assistants to do that for you.

An inexpensive place to get your newsletter template done is on a website called E-lance. That's www.elance.com. There you can hire a contractor and you can put up a job and say, 'This is what I'm after. This is my branding.' Then you hire whoever you like based on their portfolio or what they have done.

Once again, newsletters are a form of appreciation marketing. In your newsletters, your intention shouldn't be to sell, sell, sell. You might sell every third or fourth newsletter and tell people of an upcoming event or a release of a new product. However, your newsletter, just like a social media enterprise, is there to add value to people. You're there to educate people. Nowadays it's about education-based marketing, not about being salesy.

So educate, educate, educate. How is it that you can make their life easier and provide a solution to their problem?

A lot of people say to us, 'What if I give away my best stuff in my newsletter, and then people won't come and buy my product or service?' That's the wrong type of mindset to have. What you need to remember is that if people see what your best stuff is; then they'll start thinking, 'What will I get if I pay for that person to help me out?'

Always, always give away your best stuff. That is the way to amazing sales and unprecedented business growth.

Both with sending out cards and newsletters, you need to have systems behind these. You need to know when you're doing them and how you go about doing them. So remember to put together a system. Are you going to decide that each of your clients will get a card when they come on board? When they have a birthday? When it's Easter and it's Christmas time? What times of the year will you send those things out so that if you do get a virtual assistant as such to help you out, they know to do that for you, and then that particular task gets taken off your hands?

Same thing: decide on your newsletter frequency and in the week that it will go out, systemize it. Write the step-by-step process. And then this is another job you can hand over to someone when you get really, really busy.

Ultimately at the end of the day, we're hoping that you will be too busy to do these types of things. We want you to be too busy to do Facebook marketing. We want you to be too busy to send out cards and write newsletters. But to get to that point, you first have to start doing those things yourself and then pass them on to someone else because you're the one who knows your business most intimately. You're the only one who can come up with the systems of how someone can replicate what you have done before.

Once you have systemized your business, it's so much easier to hand that job or role over to someone else. That's where you stop selling your time for money and you start working smarter and not harder.

So how do we know that appreciation marketing works? Easy. You test and measure. What is the response that you get, perhaps to your newsletters? Or are people really appreciative of your cards? You will get texts and messages that say, 'Thank you so much for sending that card. That's really lovely' or 'That's really thoughtful, I love it. Thank you so much.'

When you see people showing you appreciation for the effort

you have gone to send them a card, know that it's working because they see you in a positive light. If they see you in a positive light, if they don't come purchase from you, perhaps they will think of someone who is in need of your services or products. With the newsletters, we have often found that people come back to us six, twelve, eighteen months after they have been on our newsletter database list and said, 'Thank you so much for sending out all those newsletters. I love reading them each time and I'm now ready to come and buy a service or a product.'

It happens. It doesn't happen overnight. Don't expect it to be a magic bullet that will bring in business the minute you send out a newsletter or the minute you post out a card. Again, the key is consistency. Anything in business, especially when you are new in the first couple of years, is about consistently doing things over and over and over again so that people realize you are serious about being in business. It proves that you're not just another person who opens their doors and shuts in twelve months' time.

We know those percentages are huge, that over ninety percent of businesses will close down within the first twelve months. This is partly because they haven't been consistent in their first year. They haven't put together any systems. Perhaps they haven't managed their cash flow correctly and a big, big reason why a lot of businesses fail in the first twelve months is because of their poor mindset.

A mindset expecting that all their hard work will be repaid within a few months' time and then everything will be okay. Not necessarily. I mentioned the figures earlier in the book of how the Red Ninja earned only $7,000 in her first year, $41,000 the second year. Those are not even someone's annual salary. However, she worked over sixty hours every week consistently for the first two years so that she cracked the six-figure income mark and now going full steam ahead toward seven figures.

It's not a quick fix. You do have to be patient. And in the meantime if you do need to take a day job to cover some of your expenses and to put food on the table, that's perhaps what you need to do. In the background, however, you still need to be spending a certain amount of time working on your business and letting people know that you are also a business.

A bonus tip we would like to add here for you is what Donna and Natasa do on a regular basis. And they do it every day. They always do their best to tell at least one new person about their business and that's what they did from Day One. Wherever they go whether it is the bank teller or the courier that comes over to deliver something at the house, whoever it is that they meet at a social event or a party they tell about their businesses

They ask first, 'What do you do?' And they speak to the person, and then once you've heard that about the other person, the general law of reciprocity says that the other person will ask you back about you. 'Well, what do you do?' And then you have an opportunity to let them know in a short sixty seconds what we like to call the barbeque speech. What would you say to a person what you do if you were around a barbeque?

So let's recap what this chapter is about. This chapter is to teach you how to use appreciation marketing from the couch in your business. It really is something that makes you stand above so many other businesses. Because us being in business and then watching how other businesses relate to their customers – because we're surrounded by businesses all the time.

We're using a business probably five times a day, if not more? It's really interesting to be an outsider and look at how they operate and what they do for their customers. This is one of the things that we noticed that sets amazing businesses apart from the mediocre businesses is appreciation marketing. This is because they know how important it is to build their relationship with a client and also to deliver amazing value even before they get paid.

Use appreciation marketing. Set yourself up on SendOut-Cards. Also, start a regular newsletter. If you can't do one a fortnight, do one a month. One a month is still keeping you top of mind with your customer.

What is the first company that comes to your mind when you say a soft drink? I bet you it is Coca-Cola. That is where you want to end up for your clients. When they say a solution for a specific problem, you want your business to come up to the top of their mind. That's what appreciation marketing does.

In the next chapter, we're going to talk about the power of webinars, another form of Ninja Couch marketing to allow you to spread the word about your business right from the comfort of your own home through online seminars.

Chapter 6
The Awesome Power of Webinars

Sharing your expertise far and wide has become so much easier nowadays. That is what Ninja Couch Marketing is all about.

In this chapter, we would love to discuss with you how you can expand your business globally through the power of webinars.

What is a webinar? A webinar is an online seminar. People log in, they register and then participate at the time of the call.

There's a really cool program that we use called GoToWebinar. This program is not free. There is a monthly subscription however, there is a thirty-day free trial if you would like to give it a go and run your very first webinar for profit.

They're so amazing for marketing your business because you don't have to leave your house to explain to people the amazing value that you can deliver through the problem that you solve. People can actually hear you and get a feel for what you're about and receive value beyond the asking price.

Actually, the best way to market webinars is to do them for free. Everyone loves freebies. Therefore, what you will be able to do through running webinars is get people to experience your services or products prior to them signing up or purchasing from you. This is something that hasn't been tapped into by many businesses. However, lots of entrepreneurs out there do them time and time again.

Ninja Business Chicks, as well as many other brands, run regular monthly or a six-weekly webinars just to teach people our golden knowledge, totally for free. We know if we give them our best stuff, as we discussed in the previous chapters, people will want to find out more. They want to be part of the community. They will want to hang out with you and invest in what other goods and services you have to offer.

Another great thing about webinars is that they're an instant product creation. It's something that you can record. You can upload it on YouTube and have it posted on your website so that it sells for you time and time and time again. It's amazing.

Once you've done a series of webinars, you might like to package them up. You might like to extract the audio from the webinar and actually deliver it as a product or a program. For example, Ninja Business Chicks is doing a $10 podcast. We have a community of people who have come on board and like to receive an hour from Natasa and Donna each month with a whole lot of different action tips to enable them to grow their business. We like to say "explode" their business and this podcast is only $10 a month. So at the end of those 12 months, when we have recorded it, what we can do to really leverage our intellectual property is to sell it as a program. A twelve-step program or a twelve-week program however we want to do it.

Through doing recordings, webinars, workshops, everything that you do we advise that you record it. The leverage that you can actually achieve through these products is amazing not only is it advertising on YouTube, it's advertising on your website and it's creating products that you can sell for profit.

I would love for you to take away this point. Get yourself a video recorder. Make sure that you always record everything that you do. When people, for example, miss the webinar – say you have one hundred people register, most likely fifty percent of those will turn up live on the call. What happens to the other fifty percent who actually missed out on that call? If you can supply the recording and they can watch it in the comfort of their home whenever they have time, you still have a potential of making extra sales once they have heard the recording.

It's an amazing platform to upsell to a bigger program, package and products so that people receive the free value, but then they know what the next steps are. As we know, you cannot solve a person's problem in just 60 minutes and you know what? It's a great way to boost your confidence and certainty in what you have to offer.

Maybe the early webinars you run won't be so crash hot. We remember back at our first one. The Red Ninja, when she did her very first one, she had it scripted from A to Z. She actually read out the whole content. Nowadays we just rock up, we put the computer on, we have our PowerPoint ready and we start talking. We're very interactive, very natural with our audience. However, in the early days, that wasn't the case and it's okay for it to be hard and to be scripted in the early days, as long as you go out there and do it. The important thing is that you are taking action.

So I want to teach you a little bit about what an awesome webinar is and how you can set it up. How can you promote it? What are the steps to take so you can run them successfully? If you can make this work from the couch, you won't need to leave your house to actually sell thousands of dollars of product.

Recently the Red Ninja ran a webinar that thirty people attended. That's not a high number. We've had over one hundred people register for our webinars. So even though thirty people attended it resulted in $30,000 in sales in the three weeks following that particular webinar.

So what is an awesome webinar? It's about the audience and engaging them and making it fun. Including the participants and telling them to ask any questions along the way and importantly answering all of their questions. Really serving that audience that's at the other end of the call the best way you possibly can around what they need and what they want.

You want to be professional and organized and to welcome everyone. You want to make sure they can hear you, they can see you and they know how to use their question box and it's about having an irresistible offer at the very end. An irresistible offer, because if you don't sell them the next step, and they have loved what you have delivered in this particular webinar, guess what? They're going to find it somewhere else.

Also, it's about incentivizing, so if you do have an irresistible offer, it's for those people who have taken the time to attend the call live, or perhaps they are listening to the recording, that you can give them a nice discount or add some bonuses.

A nice tip that I want to share is that giving away two value-adding bonuses is always a great way to go. When you do run a free webinar, I say have one intention in mind. Don't offer fifty million different services and products. Have one intention and up-sell to one thing that you want them to take action on. Otherwise you're starting to blur what your message is and what you want that person to do at the other end of the call.

Use some scarcity tactics. The law of scarcity; 'Ten people can get this product at X amount of dollars. The rest will pay this much.' This also brings in the urgency to people taking up the offer. They're all marketing strategies and something that you can implement when you are talking to people.

Be very organized. Plan how things will go and have an intention to have an amazing time ahead. We always set goals prior to a webinar we run. 'Okay, so this is what our offer is. This is how we plan that this webinar will run and the results that we would ideally like to get are X, Y and Z' and we put those down as measurables. We write down the statistics. How many people would we love to have live on the call? How are we going to follow up? And what are the numbers or what are the dollars we would like to come out of hosting a free webinar?

Next I would like to share with you the top five secrets of how to run your first webinar for profit.

Secret No. 5: The Sexy Name

We have spoken about this in the previous chapters. What you want to do is when you create the name of your webinar, you want to make sure that you rouse a lot of curiosity in the people who you invite to come along in terms of what you will deliver in it.

Recently The Ninjas ran their webinar called "Ninja Business Strategies: For Profit In Your Home-Based Business." So there are a few different hypnotic words in there: "profit" and "strategies." Even a home-based business appeals to a specific niche. It's not just for any business. Our target market is home-based businesses and we want to teach them how to market from their couch.

So the sexy name is super important, and again, what do people want? People want more money. More time. More freedom. So in the title of that webinar, that is what we were promising. Did we give people what they needed? Yes. We told people how they can plan. How they can market themselves. How they can leverage and how they can be seen as the credible expert in their niche. That is what we taught people in the webinar and they walked away with amazing value from a free hour that they spent with us.

Did some people end up taking action and taking on our irresistible offer at the end? Absolutely. Because they loved what we delivered. We were there to serve them and yes, they took action and we made profit out of running a free webinar right from the comfort of our own couch.

So make sure that your webinar has a sexy name, and that it oozes what people want. Again, people want easy, fast and simple. They want more money and they want more time and freedom in their lives. They want a lifestyle. That is what you need to sell them. When you come on the call, you give them what they need because ultimately they're coming on the call to find out what is it that you can share with them that will give them those things in their life.

It will never be a magic word; however, the title or the name of your webinar will need to ooze that it's that magic, quick fix. Marketing 101.

Secret No. 4: The Marketing of Your Webinar.

There's a few different ways that you can market your webinar. And as we mentioned in Chapter 1, Marketing 101, there are two ways of marketing: online and offline. In the early days of business, you might find them more successful by speaking to people offline about your webinars, especially if you don't have too many connections on the social media platforms.

What you can do is tell people when you go out networking. Tell your family and friends if they have someone they know. And e-mail your database, no matter how many people you have. Maybe in your initial webinars, you'll only have five, six people turn up. Certainly that has happened to us. With consistency and over a longer period of time when we established ourselves as experts in our chosen niches, nowadays our webinars pull numbers such as seventy-five, 124. We haven't lately had a webinar where less than fifty people have registered.

The name has a lot to do with it, but also, when you achieve a certain credibility and expertise in your business, that is where you also will find that you have a higher pull from social media.

That's not to say not to advertise your event early on in social media. What you want to do is set up an event on Facebook. Put up the registration links. Put a little bit about what people walk away with by attending that call with you. That also has to ooze sexy stuff. Hypnotic words and selling people what they want: Three key things they'll walk away with when they have listened to your webinar.

Send a list to your database. See if you can even tap into another person's business list. If there is a business that is not in competition with you – however, they have your target market, then see if you can approach them and say, 'Hey, I'm running this free webinar. Do you think the people on your list would be interested in coming along and listening to something for free?' It could be a gift that the business owner actually passes on to their list because it is valuable content. So don't be scared to ask. What's the worst thing that will happen? So what if people say no. At the end of the day it's better to have tried and failed than not to have tried at all.

Also in social media, rather than just posting an event, you might also like to put up little comments. Letting people know on your fan page that the event is coming up, and when you have set up the event, to post people little updates of what's happening. There's going to be exciting things coming up. Give them a little tease every time you post in that event as they'll get a notification. And then that reminds them that they have been invited to an event that possibly they would benefit from. So if they haven't clicked "going," they'll go back and re-visit it and go, 'Oh, actually I do want to go to that particular event.'

Really, really powerful stuff. So posting on your fan page and posting on your normal news feed is very important. Not every single day so you then become repetitive however, give yourself a two-week lead-in time. That's our suggestion in terms of webinars. Don't plan them six weeks ahead of time because webinars are so instant and in the comfort of people's homes rather than workshops that you see face-to-face people. The difference is, when you see people face-to-face, I would give six weeks lead-in of promotion. When it's webinars, even seven to ten days is enough to entice and get people excited about attending this particular call. It's very, very powerful.

So remember, online and offline marketing are the way to go, and then you get people's contact details, you can add them onto your database, and then even if they don't buy from you right then and there, remember what we said in the previous chapter. Appreciation marketing. You keep talking to them through your newsletters and you invite them to other things, say maybe a different content webinar.

Sometimes people take a little bit longer. They have what we like to call in the mindset field: their convincer strategy. Some people are convinced after one time. Some people, two or three times. And some people many times convincers, so remember that. Sometimes you won't sell something on the first go, but if you keep in touch with that person and they are a two or three time or a many time convincer, they will come back to you and purchase from you in the future because you have kept in touch.

So a great way to boost your database list is by hosting free webinars.

Secret No. 3: The Format System

This is the system that the Red Ninja learned through the coaching school where she went to learn how to run a successful workshop. It's a very easy way to structure a webinar. The format system goes through the *why*, the *what*, the *how* and the *what if*.

The why is where you deliver the benefits. Why are people listening to you? What will they walk away with by spending this hour with you online? What are all the benefits out of all the information you're about to share with them? This is where you deliver that.

Then you go into the what. What will you be talking about tonight? Perhaps if there's three key points you want to address, you might have a PowerPoint slide there saying, 'Tonight we will be addressing X, Y and Z' or '1, 2 and 3.'

Then you go into the how. Then you start off into each point. And when you start off into each point, you will go into the why. Why is it important to know about the first point? What is the first point and how can you give people the tools they need to do their particular strategy or whatever it is that you're teaching?

Then you stop at the very end and you do the what-if. A Q&A time. Are there any queries, concerns, comments? What have they learned? What have they noticed? What would they like to share? You give a pause and you wait for some comments, or you encourage people to post their questions as they are going along as that will make everything flow a lot easier than waiting at the other end in silence.

On webinars, it feels like you're waiting a long time if you're waiting for five seconds in silence, so it's good to encourage people to post up their comments and questions a lot earlier than when you stop talking and can actually start reading through them. It's great to read out comments and questions out loud so everyone else can then hear it, and then you're paraphrasing and explaining what you're actually answering. Then you move on to your second point and you go through the format system again: the why, the what, the how and Q&A time, which is the 'what if.'

At the very end of the webinar, always be very respectful of everyone's time. Finish on time. Say to your attendees that you will finish on time however, if they have any unanswered questions, you'll stick around for ten to fifteen minutes afterwards to answer those. The content will be delivered within the promised time frame. Always, always be respectful of that because people will appreciate it and see you as an integral business owner.

Secret No. 2: How to Get Organized

Getting organized for a webinar is a lot easier than getting organized for a face-to-face workshop or seminar that you might run. All you would need to think about, and you would need to create a system – once again, we're back at systems – you need to create a system for how you promote your webinar, how you invite people, when you create posts to remind people that this is coming up, and also your PowerPoint presentations.

What will you show in your PowerPoints? Our suggestion is to mix up words with pictures and have a picture within the slide as well as words. Don't make your PowerPoint slides too text-heavy because it's not about reading from them. It's about just using them as a guide. Where to next?

We like to use a picture within every slide that sort of explains what the slide is about because we understand that there are some visual people, there are some auditory people and there are some kinesthetic people. So get the slides happening and make them nice and clear. They'll guide you when you need to be talking and after all, once you know your content really well, you can just talk very naturally.

It does take practice, so make sure that you practice, practice, practice. If you have to run your webinar all on your own to just make sure that you have all the content in place, do exactly that. As I said, we had webinars scripted in the early days so that we wouldn't say a lot of ums and stop and feel flustered and unprofessional. Nowadays they just run so smoothly and easily.

When you're certain and confident, your audience will end up connecting with you and wanting to interact with you. So remember, in the early days you might feel, 'Oh, no one's talking! They don't like me!' That fear of not being good enough pops up. However, delivering certainty and confidence is so, so powerful because then people just see you as that expert and they will ask you the question and trust that you know what you will answer.

So remember a point that I've said earlier. Everything is hard before it becomes easy.

Secret No. 1: Test and Measure

Make sure that you have an irresistible offer. Have a special price for being on the call. Have some bonuses. Two bonuses are awesome when you run a webinar.

Ask for feedback. Usually people will give it to you at the end of the call or you may like to e-mail them. What would you like to know about next time? Is there something that wasn't covered that you're interested in knowing? This is how you come up with content for future webinars.

It's so, so easy to get the feedback about what people want because that's actually what you need to sell to them. Sell to these people what they want and asking these people who are on your calls what they would like to know about in the future will help you create your new content.

Measure how your sales went. Measure how many people were there. What is the percentage of people? Is there more follow-up needed leading up to the calls so that you ensure more live participants are on the call?

Always, always go back. If something's not working, remember the old saying, *If you're doing the same thing over and over and expecting a different result, then that's the definition of insanity.*

Webinars can be an amazing tool for your business. Remember, use them and remember that the numbers you attract to your webinars will grow the longer you are in business. Start them today, though. If you're practicing on five or six people, that's OK. We even once did a webinar for two or three people as you have to start somewhere and then that'll grow.

Enjoy them. Do them. It's one of the most powerful couch marketing strategies that gets people into your world, into your business and puts you on a platform as being an expert and someone who will help them solve the problem that they have, whatever your niche may be.

Chapter 7
Boosting Your Business Via Forums

Earlier on, you would've read a little bit about positioning yourself as a leader in your industry, the power that it holds and the way it can grow your bottom line.

When people think about promoting themselves and growing their business using online marketing techniques, many of you probably haven't thought about forums (and the benefit and growth that forums can bring) including the way it can help you grow as a leader in your industry.

For those of you who don't know, the best way to describe a forum is simply as an online discussion.

It gives you the capacity to talk with other people on similar topics where you can comment on each other's conversations, start new threads of conversation and interact with other members.

Every time you comment on a thread or a conversation, a little image or gravatar of who you are will pop up next to your comment. This forms part of your signature and your little profile image and your name, which is where the power comes in. But more of that later on.

First thing's first. What you want to do is determine what kind of forums you want to join. There are free forums and there are paid forums. Free forums are fantastic because obviously they are free. They don't cost you anything and you can really get your head around how forums work, which is a very good tip if you've never interacted in a forum before. It'll teach you about the technology, how they work and how the flow of conversation works.

You will also learn about forum etiquette. You may or may not be aware but most forums are quite strict about what you can and cannot say.

For example, usually you cannot say anything about your business or promote yourself and your services. You usually cannot use it as a sales technique. Forums are there as a way to share information and collaborate with people. It's a medium for discussing topics. It is a way of learning and sharing and growing. So I'm sure you're sitting there thinking, 'Well how is this a benefit to me if I can't even sell?' Read on and we will let you know.

The other type of forum is the paid variety. Now paid forums generally speaking, have a higher-caliber of member that you can interact with, because simply they've paid. People value the content that they're learning from there and are happy to pay for it. They want to talk in greater detail about better and valuable topics (rather than a chat room when it could be about general life). It's not a place for trolling (making fun of people) or where you just send jokes and have a chat about what you did on the weekend. As they're paid forums on a particular topic or industry, generally speaking, it has better quality conversation that people are interacting and participating in.

Both options are fantastic, and it's a matter of finding the right one where you fit. There are two ways you can look at it. You can look at finding a forum online in a particular industry that you're in. For example, Donna supports people who are starting and growing their own virtual assistant business.

Or you can go down the path of markets. So knowing your target market is very important if you want to go down this path. By understanding exactly who your client is and what they like to talk about you will then be able to make a more informed decision on where they are hanging out (and what they like to talk about).

Although Donna often talks about starting and growing your own virtual assistant business, one of Donna's main target markets are stay-at-home mums. So she could possibly select a forum that has that target market of stay-at-home mums.

Highly likely those forums will be about cooking, cleaning, looking after the kids, craft activities and recipes and things about that nature, but highly likely, one of the topics of conversation that will pop up is working from home and how to earn a little bit of extra money. As a stay-at-home mum, you're usually living on one wage so earning money from home is a common discussion. We know this because Donna understands her target market REALLY well. This is a great example of **getting into your clients mind** and understanding what their needs and wants are.

To recap you can search industry forums or find one where your target market hangs out.

These are the two ways you can go when you're deciding on what type of forum you can possibly join. We recommend that you do one of each if you possibly can even for a short while so you can see the difference and where you fit the best. If you've got the time and the capacity to interact with both, then go for it, but if you have only got the time to support one avenue, then it is probably better that you interact with people in your target market rather than in your industry depending on what you do.

The reason why we say this, going back to Donna's example, is that when she interacts on the forums, her profile name is "WorkFromHomeQueen." She may comment on recipes and children's activities and cleaning tips and anything of that nature, because she can't promote what she actually does. But any time a topic of conversation comes up surrounding working from home, she can be very careful and just comment on a broad nature of various areas of topics that would steer people in her direction.

The more time and effort that you put in educating people, helping answer any questions you know the answer to and just interacting with people, the more times that your profile pops up. In turn the more likely people are going to click on your profile page and see who you are and what you do.

'Who is this person? Who is this WorkFromHomeQueen? She always seems to be commenting on things. I'm going to go check her out and see what she does.' These are the questions that run through member's heads, which is why they will go out and search more. It's human nature – we are curious about people so lets make it easy for them to find out more about your awesome product or service.

You might be wondering, 'Why would I join a forum if I can't advertise?' Well in your signature (that pops up with each comment you leave), you're effectively **marketing yourself**. Forums do allow signatures (which are very similar to an e-mail signature) and it's here you can have links to your Facebook page, your website or you can even have a link to a YouTube video. The options are endless and the choice is yours – can you see how this is where it can get powerful!

You see, what we're doing here is positioning you as a **leader in your industry**. So Donna might be a leader in the virtual assistant industry with stay-at-home moms. And if her profile keeps popping up every day, answering questions and interacting with people, and they see her little signature saying, *'More info about working from home,'* then what do you think is going to happen? People are going to click on it, which will take them to her page, and that's where they can connect with her directly and learn more about what she does. This will ensure that she doesn't break any forum rules and allows her to actually interact personally with those people who are genuinely interested in learning more (as they sought her out).

But if she was to blatantly go out and say, *'Hey, check it out. This is what I do. I want you to buy my product. Here's the price,'* forum administrators, the people that manage the forum, will block her and delete her out of their system, because that's not what forums are for. They're not for areas of selling. They're platforms for sharing knowledge.

If a third person actually found Donna's content valuable and they really liked it, they're more than welcome to say, *'Hey, I've actually trialed this product. It was pretty cool. You should check it out. Here's the link.'* Most forum administrators would actually allow that type of comment or conversation because it's not coming from you. It's a testimonial; in this case someone who has tested the product.

Therefore forums are an amazing way for you to actually build your credibility in your industry or your target market in a particular topic or a niche area that you're working on.

The key important parts here are look for free and paying forums that work into your budget. Can you afford this paid forum? If you're going to use a paid forum, make sure you make the most of it and actually interact on it. Don't just sit there thinking, 'I'll just interact when I can,' because obviously then you're paying money for something that's not worth it.

If it's a free forum, be careful of people trolling or jokes. Don't get pulled into the chitter-chatter. Just always deliver really good content, really good feedback and really good tips and advice.

Where can you find forums? Well, quite easily, it's a matter of Googling the word "forum" with a particular topic. So it might be cooking forums. It might be baby forums. It might be mum forums. It might be Melbourne or Sydney forums if you're in Australia. You've just got to do a little bit of research and you'll be able to easily find these forums that you could possibly interact with.

We know we've mentioned this already, but really they are a powerful tool to really position yourself as an industry leader (we just want to make sure you get it!).

We know Donna is part of a forum for virtual assistants that she interacts with and here is an awesome example of how positioning and sharing can lead to business growth.

There is a particular person on this forum who is very knowledgeable on WordPress. Every time someone posts a question regarding WordPress such as, 'How do I do this?' or 'How do I do that?' She is often one of the first people (or only person) who knows how to answer the question and solve the problem. She has shared her knowledge for so long that she is now the **go-to** WordPress person.

As such, internally, people have hired her for WordPress support because she has positioned herself that way and she's built up her credibility in that niche. Ultimately she is the 'go-to' person for WordPress. NOW if any members of the forum meet someone out in the public looking for a WordPress go-to person, she will be the first that they think of and probably refer to.

Remember, at the end of the day, everything that we're sharing here in Ninja Couch Marketing is all about building your credibility. This is about who you are and what you do, especially the knowledge that you have, because ultimately this is what will enable you to **charge more and sell more,** which will enable you to make more money at the end of the day.

This particular marketing technique, like all of our techniques, can be completed simply on the couch. You can jump on at night, check out the conversations that have been happening, and interact and comment where you want, or you can do it throughout the day. One of the biggest tips that we can share with you is that you must make it a habit to interact VERY regularly, a minimum of four times a week, preferably daily –

so we're not talking about a set and forget technique. This one takes time and dedication.

A really good tip that we can share with you is about managing your interaction and time spent. When you join a forum, you usually use your email address as your username. You create your profile page with your photo or your logo and your signature and your contact details, and any relevant links. You will always use an e-mail address to log in and your e-mail address is where you will receive every single notification from a forum.

So if you start a conversation or if you join a conversation, because you've commented on a topic, you will get an e-mail in your inbox every time another comment is added (unless you set up your options not to do so, but that kind of defeats the purpose). You'll always get notified when somebody has participated in a conversation you are also participating in very similarly to Facebook.

Because that could get quite onerous, particularly if you're in a very active forum, it is advised that you should probably create a separate e-mail address. A lot of people create an e-mail address with a business name, for example, forums@ninjabusinesschicks.com.au, which can be used for multiple forums and other groups you may participate in.

You can create that as a secondary e-mail address so that you can get those e-mails separately from your normal e-mails via a different inbox. Or you can set up a rule in your mail program, whether it's Mail or Outlook or Gmail, etc, that any e-mails that come from this address need to go into a particular folder. So any e-mails that come from the forum address (because it'll have the forum name in the e-mail) go in your selected folder. This way your inbox is not getting bombarded with potentially hundreds of e-mails that can distract you from work (or simply overwhelm you). You can then quickly scroll through and find the ones that are appropriate to you and you'd want to actually interact with and comment on.

So just to recap once again, our top tips are

- find some forums.

- do some research.

- try out a free forum if you've never interacted on a forum before, just so you can get the feeling of how it goes and what's the etiquette and language and technology and what it's like.

- make sure your signature is up to date and you've got links that work to your appropriate pages. If you want it to go to your Facebook page, pop it in. If you want it to go to your website or any other page, pop it in.

- start to interact and share with other members!

Now, as a bonus tip (because who doesn't like a bonus), what you really should do is anyone who you ever interact with quite considerably and that you seem to be growing quite closely with, find them on Facebook if you can and connect with them personally. That way you can talk and interact one-on-one without having to be in the forum area.

That is a big, big tip that you can apply to every chapter. Whatever technique you're using to interact with people, find that person on Facebook and friend them if you can. Ultimately it's their choice whether they accept it or not, but don't wait for them to get the ball rolling. If they accept awesome, if they don't it doesn't matter. Don't be offended as some people really keep Facebook just for personal interactions.

If they have a business page and you like what they do, "like" their business page as well so they can see that you're doing that. It all builds credibility and starts to build loyalty. It all boosts the relationship that you are building with this particular person. You will see in time people will start speaking your name and sharing your links and talking about you because, hey, we just proved to everyone that you seem to know quite a lot and seem to be quite helpful to people (which is fantastic!).

Being seen as a very helpful, generous, sharing person is amazing for your business. It doesn't mean you need to give away free advice. But if someone asks you (if you're a hairdresser), *'What is the best type of product do I need to use for this particular type of hair,'* and you shared that tip which took you thirty seconds, that is far more powerful than charging someone for your time to come and do their hair, because what you're putting in here is positioning yourself as a leader and the go-to expert in your industry.

Some of you may be reading this and considering the possibility of starting your own forum. This is definitely something that you can consider at any point in running your business, and the positioning power that comes from running your own forum is extremely powerful. People look to you as a leader and they look to you for advice and guidance, as it is your responsibility to manage the comments and everything that is going through your forum. As you can imagine, this really puts you apart from everyone else. But there are some drawbacks.

Unless you have enough people interacting on your forum and you've got quite a lot of people coming along and joining and talking, it won't work. So forums can be quite difficult to get started unless you have enough interest. If you've already established quite a heavy network of contacts within your industry that you regularly talk to, potentially by e-mail or Facebook, then starting a forum might actually work for you.

A simple forum could be in the form of a Facebook group. And we've talked about Facebook earlier on, but just as an example, it doesn't have to be a traditional forum with a traditional forum structure. This forum could simply be a Facebook group that you're interacting and talking with.

When starting a forum you would naturally start a free one because it's very hard to charge people for a forum where there are three members and little interaction. So sometimes it can take a lot of time to get it going. A lot of time that is taking you away from potential income earning activities in the short term. Therefore forums should always be treated as a long-term project.

If you get big enough and you have a lot of people talking on your forum, you will really need a moderator. You can always hire moderators to make sure that the content is appropriate and no one's doing anything inappropriate, such as selling or using explicit language, but still you have to manage that forum. Overall, it's your responsibility to make sure that everything is tip-top and a-okay.

So if you're sitting there thinking, 'Should I start my own forum?' we're definitely not discouraging you from doing it, but if your ultimate goal is to build your own business and your own bottom line, then really consider what are the reasons that you want to start your forum. Maybe you love talking on forums and it's fun, but is it going to achieve the goal of growing your main business? Possibly not, so really take a sit-down and think before you start your own one, what is your intention and what you're really trying to achieve by doing it.

In summary, we want you to put the effort in to become the go-to expert in your industry or to your target market. Become the known one in your group for always having the answers for those difficult questions. For sharing knowledge and for being a real leader in your industry. Always promote yourself without getting banned and be smart about how you do it. Also HAVE FUN!

Chapter 8

Magnetize Your Customers Via Video

Ah, YouTube.

Some people love it. Some people hate it.

And guess what? If you're a business owner and you want to market yourself from the couch, you're going to love it. And if you don't yet, you will soon.

Everybody knows what YouTube is. YouTube is a platform that gives you the ability to host videos of your choice that you can then share with your community. Sharing can be as simple as telling people about it, or sharing on your Facebook page. You can embed it into your website and include links on your e-mail signature. It's just an amazing tool to promote your business ... and it's FREE!

We know it can be hard for small home-based businesses to spend money on marketing, so YouTube is the perfect medium to get your brand out there to a wider market.

There are millions and millions of videos on YouTube. Why has this happened, why has it exploded and why do businesses benefit from this? The reason is consumers, (every day ordinary people) love to connect with people one-on-one if they can.

Similarly, from the other angle – depending on your personality type – people love to be famous and often YouTube is the only platform they have to get their name out there.

However, from a business perspective, consumers LOVE to get to know their brands, friends and idols to find out about their world and what they are doing.

When consumers can watch what you are doing and saying (especially your face), you will get a stronger connection than if they're just reading your content or listening to you speak.

If you share podcasts or audio recordings, it's still pretty cool and a great way to connect with others in your community. Especially for those who are audio learners (prefer to listen than do or see), however if they can see your face while you're doing it, people will make a stronger connection to you (and the stronger connection, the more likely these fans will become your customers).

They want to know more about your offering.

They want to know about what you're doing.

They want to learn about who you are.

If you're interesting to watch and you give great information, consumers are more likely to keep an eye out for your future videos and start to follow what you do and what you're offering.

There are a few tricks of the trade when you're using video as a promotional tool in your business. You need to keep it interesting and do lots of different things. Repetitive videos of you talking into the camera with a white wall behind you will become very boring for your fans. Who wants to watch that every day? These two Ninjas wouldn't!

So you've got to make it interesting. Be sure to consider different backgrounds, different settings and lots of interesting content and topics.

Every video doesn't have to be in a different location, but you can be relatively interesting every time.

Always ensure your content is also varying and interesting.

This could include:

- A sale that you're offering
- An industry tip
- A piece of general information
- A resource that your fans might be interested in
- A trick that you're sharing
- A cool find that you want people to know about
- A technique that you want to share with people
- Sharing more information about what you do
- Any new services or products that you are offering
- New members to your team and other business announcements.

As you can see there are lots of different pieces of content that you can share with your fans and followers. One BIG tip that you must keep in mind is *don't always make it about sales*. Videos that are just sales spiels will soon become boring for your viewers and they will start to tune out. Sales will come after the relationship has been built and they like who you are.

Our next tip is to **keep it real**. If you fumble a little bit when you're talking, that doesn't matter. Just keep going. As long as you don't say something ridiculously wrong, just keep talking.

If an animal walks in the background into your shot, keep going. Most people love animals, so they respond really well to that. Donna does a lot of her recordings with her dog Ninja (her black Labrador) and when he walks into the videos, there is always a higher response rate to whatever she's talking about. If she's selling something, more people buy it when Ninja's in the video.

If it's just a piece of information, more people tend to share it and watch it if Ninja's in the video. She's started getting people actually contacting her and asking her when the video of Ninja's going to be, which is crazy.

The video is about her, not about Ninja. But there are people who have really connected to that and therefore remember more about who she is and what she has to offer!

This is a great example of how a connection was made with her customers and yes they came to watch her videos as she is the Work From Home Queen – but they also learned a little bit about her life, her pet (and that she is not a perfectionist and that this is normal!).

Tips When Recording Videos

1. Speak clearly.

2. Be well-presented. Unless your video is about how to look like a hobo on the couch, then don't record it like that. Look clean and tidy – you're the face of your brand. You will have heard the saying "first impressions last" and it's true.

3. Be dressed nicely or cleanly. Have makeup on if you're a lady. Do your hair, because remember, it's a first impression. If this is the first time someone's watching you and it happens to be via video rather than face-to-face, they're going to have the same first impression that they would have had if it was face-to-face, so really make sure that you take that into consideration.

4. Have a lot of natural light if you can. If you can record videos outside, it's far better than recording inside with the lights on. The colours will be better and it will be easier on the eye for viewers. There is no need to start to get big production lights, green screens and other piece of technology to make your videos. A handy cam is more than sufficient – remember they are watching YOU not thinking about how you did it!

5. Do different settings with different topics.

6. A really cool tip is people often **record a lot of videos in a row**. If you want to release a video a week, you might want to record six or seven videos in a row if they're only a couple of minutes long. This way you are being more efficient with your time.

Of course it's going to seem like you're wearing the same thing every day, but that's okay, it's not a big deal. People know that you might do that because it's more efficient. But you might move to different rooms of the house or different locations in the garden.

Which leads into my next point. **Make your videos simple and quick**.

Unless it's an instructional video, which requires quite an in-depth instruction on how to do what you're doing, (which in my opinion, then, is not really promotional – this is all about marketing yourself) then keep it short and sweet. An instructional video, a really in-depth one for ten minutes, is more of a resource video rather than a promotional one. Yes you are still promoting yourself to some degree, but for the purpose of this book we want you to make short snappy videos and lots of them!

That being said, not all instructional videos now have to be excluded. If you're doing a quick thirty-second instructional video on how to do something on your computer or how to do a quick technique on blow-drying your fringe (if your business is hairdressing), then make it quick. A two-minute maximum if you can. People do not have time to watch very long videos, particularly if your target market is business owners, or if your target market is mums. How many mums have got time to sit down and watch videos?

We're not going to harp on it too much here, but once again – it's all about positioning yourself as a leader in your industry AND in the case of videos – broaden your market to a wider audience, possibly even internationally!

Still need convincing? Hopefully not, but if so another cool reason to use YouTube is it **integrates really well in a lot of different pieces of technology**. Watching videos on your iPhone or your iPad or other smartphones is super easy and now second nature to most people.

They've been coded in to work really well on digital devices. You can embed them in your website really well. As the videos are hosted elsewhere (YouTube rather than your own server) you are making the most of an excellent resource. For if you are not aware, video files can get rather large and if you're going to host them yourself, and you've got a very small hosting account –where are they going to be stored?

It's not like people are going to be watching them right off your computer. They're going to be stored online somewhere, and this is what we mean when we talk about hosting. This is why it's cool to make the most of the free resources that are out there for you!

There is a minor downside that you need to know about YouTube. If people are watching you on the YouTube site itself (rather than an imbedded video on your website) then on the right-hand sidebar you will see there are other videos with similar search phrases available. In a way, that's a bit of competition, but that's okay. If you're giving good content and interesting videos, people will just come back to you anyway.

If people start to subscribe to your channel (which you should always encourage them to do), then they will get an automatic e-mail delivered to their inbox every time that you record a video and upload it, which is an amazing tool of leverage.

AND because Red and Purple Ninja (Nat and Donna) come

from a mindset of abundance, you should not worry about those extra videos. There is plenty for all – so if someone's watching a video about a similar topic you talk about, and then YOUR video is the competition on the right hand side – YOU could be the one to take the viewer over to your channel and site.

Okay – so that's a lot of the information about YouTube, now let's get into the nitty gritty and get you going!

When you are creating a YouTube account, try and create one in your name. Your proper name or your business name. Don't do one such as "hotchick64," because that's what you're stuck with, which means later on down the track, (even if you're not doing a business now), if you're running a business, when you post a video up, that's the account it's going to be under.

That's who people need to subscribe to, "hotchick64." Doesn't really do anything good for your positioning if you get our drift. So make sure you create an appropriate account name.

When you upload your videos, ensure that you give them an appropriate title. Remove any automatic text that your computer might put in. This could be file names, types or dates. So make sure that the file name you select is appropriate.

Ensure that you utilise the description box of the video. For every video that you upload, you have the capacity to add a description about what your video is about.

Be sure to put in a link at the beginning and a link at the end of the little description box (if you've got some text in between), back to your website, your Facebook page or wherever you want people to go. Wherever you want people to find you.

Because some people will just read the first two lines of a comment box before they have to expand it, and some people will expand it and read everything and go all the way to the end. So make sure you've got the URL that you're trying to drive people to both at the beginning of your text box and at the end of your text box.

Ensure that the URL you are sharing is not just to your homepage. Be sure to include other links to other areas of your website. It might be various backlinks for various different pages, and sub pages. Those deep, embedded pages actually boost your search-engine optimization and your Google ranking, which will mean that you come up higher when people search for keywords that your website is well-known for.

So don't always include the URL just to your homepage on your YouTube videos or even in your forum signature and other areas that we're going to talk about. Make sure you use other URLs within your website. Deep set back-links that will boost your website overall and will boost your credibility.

Make use of the tags fields. Tags are key words that add to the description of your video that help people to find you. So if we're recording a video on our book, "Ninja Couch Marketing," we might put tags in such as "ninja," "couch," "marketing," the whole phrase "ninja couch marketing," because people type it in different ways. We would put key phrases in such as "Donna Brown" and "Natasa Denman," because we're the authors. We might put in "ninja business chicks," because people might find us that way.

So think logically. If I want someone to find me, what will they type in? Well they'd probably type in "ninja business chicks."

They may type in "Natasa" or "Donna." They may type in the title of the book. They may just type in "marketing from home" because they don't know who we are and don't know our business name.

They could be from another country, but they are interested in learning about marketing from home. So if you put in all these key words in the tags, you have a higher chance of people finding your video when they do that particular search. So make use of tags. A lot of people don't make use of tags, but make sure YOU make use of tags. It's one of our Ninja tips.

Also, make sure that you utilize all areas that YouTube has to offer. For example did you know that you can add a transcription of your video? If you are speaking for two minutes about a particular topic, and it's awesome content (because we know that's what you will be doing), then you can put a little transcription of that audio, into the transcription box that's available to all account holders in the advanced settings.

Google will often search the transcription box far more than the description box. They may search just the title of your video, but not necessarily the comments box. But they do search the transcription box. Therefore this increases your search-engine optimization, or SEO. It makes it easier for Google to find you when people are searching using your tags and key words. Definitely take advantage of that. It's a little trick that not many people are doing, so we're very keen to share it with you!

Once you've created your video and you've uploaded it, ensure that you share it with all the appropriate channels. Put it on your Facebook page. Put it on your website if you've got the capacity to share videos. Learn how to do it if you don't know how to do it. There are lots of people out there who know how to do it. Or ask us how to do it and we can help teach you.

Include links in your newsletters or any other material that you share with people if that's how you want to position yourself as a real gun in what you do.

One aspect that is highly important in our opinion is to make sure that the video looks clean. Don't just have raw footage that you've just recorded and uploaded and you haven't cleaned it up. Unless you are positioning yourself as a construction worker who is doing videos on the fly in the dust and mud, so you might have quite raw footage because it doesn't seem right that if you're putting in all these cool, fancy headings with start and end jingle music.

But if you are working in an office and you want to position yourself as a professional then you might want to have a little intro slide, which could just be simply a solid-colour screen with the title of the video merging into the beginning of the video.

All these little things just make it seem a little bit nicer and a little bit cleaner and make people watch a little bit longer.

Unless you're getting hundreds of thousands of people watching your videos, avoid putting advertisements on your videos. It actually is quite frustrating for a lot of people. A lot of people don't like them. But they understand that this is how people make their money on YouTube, and this is how YouTube makes their money as well. Every time you see an ad on a YouTube video, or you click on one of those ads, somewhere somebody got paid twenty cents, thirty cents, a dollar, depending on what the agreed value is.

So when you're getting 1.5 million hits on a video, sure add an advertisement (makes sense, we would). But if you've got only thirty people that have watched your video so far and you get one every now and then while you get your momentum going, don't use advertisements from the beginning. People will perceive that all you're interested in is making money on your videos and not actually providing really awesome content, which is what your actual goal is (or what your actual goal should be).

For those of you who are shy about video – Donna and Natasa encourage you to give it a go anyway and start to create some because videos sell really quickly. It's very easy for people to learn quite a lot of information about you and your brand in a video. Imagine if you're watching a two-minute video on someone explaining how to do something as opposed to reading written instructions. It's far, far quicker to be doing it in video form, and people learn it quicker and they love it so they can then go on to the next thing.

But so many people feel uncomfortable about it, including the Purple Ninja. Donna was very uncomfortable about recording videos when she first started, but she realized the power of it and she thought, *'You know what? Get over it. I'll just do it.'* The minute she got over it and she recorded a lot of videos, it's just exploded. It's unbelievable how many things have happened since.

We really recommend that you try and give it a go. In the final chapter of Toolkit For Success, we'll give you a lot of the technical information that you can use to help you make the most of YouTube.

But seriously, if you get over your fear, if you need to practice in the mirror what you're going to say a little bit, go for it, but don't read a script out, because reading a script is very obvious to people. You're not on a teleprompter where you can put a lot of emotion into what you're saying. Most people who read off a script will read it word for word and they can't put emotion into what they're saying.

So just wing it. If you're talking about something that you are highly knowledgeable in, which is what you should be doing, then it should come naturally to you. You shouldn't even have to think about it and you will just know what you have to say. You might have a piece of paper in front of you with a few dot points on main topic headings that you want to cover just so you don't forget anything, but you don't need to write it out word-for-word.

Its no surprise that video is the way of the future. More and more people are learning via videos and there are even schools that are teaching via video now. There are universities that are making the most of video. So it just goes to show you where society is moving towards. It is going to be one of the main ways that we are going to learn and share information, even the news so get on it today!

Many of you might be asking, 'How frequently do you need to be posting videos up on YouTube and sharing them with your network?' Well obviously this would really depend on how much time you have. You're going to learn a little bit more later on down the track in this book on your plan of attack for your couch marketing.

But if YouTube is going to be one of the key techniques that you're going to utilize in your couch marketing plan, then we recommend that you do at least two videos per week. Many people do daily videos. Many people do monthly videos. One video per week at a minimum, but two would be awesome.

Make the live time consistent if possible. Make them always on a Tuesday and a Friday, or make them always on a Saturday morning and a Wednesday, or whatever it might be. Space them out in the week so that people begin to remember when you're going to be doing them and then they'll begin to look out for them. Remember this is when they go LIVE not when you record them. You might record thirty in a day if you borrow a video camera, but they will go live on the same day every week.

Once you start having quite a lot of videos on your channel, you are then able to share a link to your channel on your Facebook page or on your website. You can even share your YouTube channel URL on any of your forum signatures.

This is all relating back to marketing from the couch. These are simple techniques that you can do from your couch and anywhere in the world so if time is an issue then they are easy enough that you can outsource them to virtual support.

The whole point of these techniques that we're sharing with you is so that if you go on holiday, if you go away, if you're working at night, wherever you might be, you can easily do these techniques and still grow your business besides the traditional networking and salsey face-to-face meetings.

So start to put some effort today and get that FAME going!

Chapter 9

Blogging Like A Pro To Increase Profits

This chapter is dedicated to blogging and the power that blogging has in marketing your business from the couch.

For those of you who don't know, blogging is a way of having an online diary or an online journal that you can put content on that you can share with people.

There are two distinct ways that blogging can contribute to your couch marketing plan:

1. Writing your own blog.

2. Commenting on other blogs.

So lets work through one, then we'll go through the other and we will show you how BOTH can help you profit from the couch! Just to let you know we are going to go over the basics of blogging in this book rather than the mechanics. We're not going to teach you about the technology (such as how to SET UP a blog, how to categorise your posts etc) as this can be easily learned online. This book is about the strategies that you can use. If you ever need help or not sure where to go for more support then you're always more than welcome to contact us for help.

We should mention that we're writing this chapter assuming that your business is not your actual blog. There are some people whose entire business is writing and maintaining a blog (where they make money from advertising) but what we're referring to is adding a blog to your existing website or online presence.

Let's start with writing your own blog. Basically it would be a dedicated page on your website where you're writing a very regular (minimum once a week) blog post that can include content such as text, videos, images, audio files that would be of value to your readership. It's about creating this awesome content on a regular basis and boosting your profile as an expert.

What you need to take into consideration here is who you are actually writing for. Who is your target market? For example, many virtual assistants write their blog based on the virtual assistant industry. They're giving tips that other VAs would benefit from.

This is not the way to go. What you want to do is write content for your target market. The people who you want to hire for you as their virtual assistant. We're using virtual assistants as the example here because that's an industry that Donna is quite familiar with.

For example, if your target market is stay-at-home mums, then what you might do is actually write some blog posts that appeal to them, but are related to your industry.

So in Donna, the purple Ninjas case, she teaches stay-at-home mums how to be virtual assistants. Though her target market is stay-at-home mums, she's not going to teach these women about recipes or cleaning, which is another area that they might be interested in, but she will write and prepare content that appeals to them that is relevant to Donna's niche and what she's actually trying to do. This might be teaching them how to find clients, how to set up a database or even how to update their own websites.

Another example might be a nutritionist who specialises in nutrition care for weight loss in overweight children, for example, or young adults – say ten, eleven, twelve-year-olds – typically the people that control their food are their parents or their teachers.

They're not going to write the article for their target market, which are children. Their target market is actually the parents, and they have to write the content that would appeal to the parents and not the children or other nutritionists.

There's no point in writing about calorie counting software or nutrition courses and programs for high socio economic families. That's inappropriate in this case. What you're trying to do is create very good content that would appeal to your target market and that might be, in this case, healthy lunch box ideas and other ways to get your child to prefer to eat vegetables rather than chocolates and sweets and other highly-processed foods. This is just an example that we're using for you to understand the type of content that you need to write and stop and think about who your actual target market is.

When you do decide to start your own blog, as mentioned earlier, you need to ensure that you are posting on it quite regularly. Minimum once a week is really the best way you're going to get lots of feedback from people. The successful blogs that are online and generate lots of interest and return on their investment of time are actually posting daily – so do keep that in the back of your mind.

Once you've written a blog, each post will have its own dedicated URL, and this URL you can share on YouTube, on your forums, on your Facebook page and other areas, even in your e-mail signature. You can share it on Twitter and other forms of social media and LinkedIn. So this is a great way to get people to back-link back to you besides your homepage, which is what we were mentioning in earlier chapters of this book.

Remember the more links back to your website BESIDES the obvious home page – the better Google will love you and the easier it will be for people to find you.

You should encourage people on your blog post to sign up to receive a notification or email every time you write a new blog post. There are tools available online that will enable you to do it automatically, so as soon as a post goes live, instantly it's fed through to their e-mail address.

They're usually called RSS feeds, and these feeds will enable you to target a lot of people very quickly with very little effort. As blogging can take a lot of time, we want you to do it as SMART and as efficient as possible.

One of the best ways to improve your brand and your positioning via blogs is to make sure that there's lots of interaction on the blog posts. Lots of comments and lots of talking and discussion about whatever the topic is that you have written will make your posts rank high in Google's opinion.

In order to do that, one of the best ways to do it is to actually ask a question. Be sure that you ask a question on a blog or request feedback from people, because this encourages people to actually interact with you.

You can run competitions. You can have tips and resources once again. You can embed your YouTube videos that we've discussed earlier.

You're probably starting to see there's a bit of a theme here, that a lot of the content that you're doing can be re-used and re-purposed, and it's something we're actually going to discuss in the following chapter about leveraging your content. But for now we're on blogs (just needed to whet your appetite a bit to keep going, hehehe).

The other type of blogging that can be an awesome Ninja Couch Marketing technique is actually commenting on other people's blogs.

This is a great way to slowly integrate into the blogging world if you're not ready to commit to writing and managing your own from the beginning.

If you find someone who is running a very interesting blog in the niche that interests you and that has a similar target market to you, then if you comment on their blog, you have the capacity to obviously leave your comment, but you always get an option to include a URL.

Once again, this is very similar to the forum concept where if you're leaving regular comments that are valuable and are providing more information or interacting in conversations, if the same people keep seeing your name pop up, then they will wonder, 'Who is this Donna that keeps commenting on this blog that I always read? She always seems to have really good comments. I'm going to go check out who she is.' And then they might click on my link and find a little bit more about me.

It's also a very good SEO technique. You can improve your search engine optimization and Google will find you easier and rank you better (aka you will come up higher in the list when someone searches you) if there are more back-links to your website. So when you're putting your URL in when you make a comment, you can put in obviously your homepage, but you can put lots of other deep back-links in for various pages that you've got or various blog posts. That also then will improve how Google finds you and ranks you. Remember what we have mentioned before – make sure you link back to other pages on your website besides the home page.

So think about who your target market is, where they hang out and where you can add value by interacting on the same blog posts. It positions you as a leader and it positions you as someone who is highly intelligent and has lots of knowledge on a topic or a field that they are interested in, so they will want to go and find out about what you know.

Readers of blogs on a topic that is similar to yours are always looking for new people to learn from and new pieces of information.

A really good technique for commenting on blogs is to ensure that you've got a Gravatar. A Gravatar is a little image that pops up wherever you put a comment in any blog. So go to Gravatar.com and create an actual Gravatar, which can be your logo or it can be a photo of yourself. This means that every time you put a comment in someone else's blog, because of the coding in the background, it'll put a little picture of whichever image you uploaded earlier, rather than you actually having their default image, which might be a silhouette of a man or a woman (or sometimes it's a little cartoon monster).

It's very easy to build up quite a lot of back-links through commenting on people's blogs. And you will see soon, if you're not careful, you will have lots of people spamming your blogs with lots of comments and links that lead to random pages that have nothing to do with you. So it's very important that you moderate the comments on your own blog and make sure that they are appropriate and from people who are genuinely interacting and commenting on the content you have given and not simply trying to create another back-link to their website.

One of the most awesome benefits of blogging is the leverage capability. You can write your content once and then benefit from the results over and over again with more people reading it, sharing it and just simply boosting you higher and higher as an authority figure.

Here are the takeaway points for running your own blog.

- Do it regularly. Once a week at a minimum.
- Keep it interesting.
- Keep your posts between 250 and 750 words on average.
- Put a variety of content including YouTube videos, audio files (such as interviews and podcasts), images, various tips and instructions or even competitions in.

So put a really big variety of the type of content you're putting in and the value that you're putting in for your target market.

- Make sure that you moderate the comments and ensure that when people are reading the comments, they are appropriate, and they're not just people who are spamming you so they can have a back-link back to their website.

And here are the takeaway points commenting on other blogs:

- Comment something relevant "great post" is too vague and won't encourage any other readers to seek you out.

- Research on what blogs are currently out there that are similar to your industry OR target market is interested in. Familiarise yourself with those who you think have great topics and content.

- Do it regularly.

- Use a Gravatar.

Blogging (as with many of these couch marketing techniques) take time to reap the results and effort must be made. A commitment to blogging will mean you get the most from this FREE powerful strategy!

Chapter 10
Time Saving Tricks Via
The Ninja Leveraging Strategy

Basically, in business, leveraging means to increase your results without having to do as much work. For example if you currently make $50,000 in sales every year, it's about getting to the $100,000 sales mark WITHOUT having to double the amount of work you do.

It is a COMPLETELY different topic on how to leverage yourself to make more direct sales, in fact you probably could write an entire book on it by itself. For the purpose of this chapter we're going to concentrate on leveraging your marketing efforts because that is what we're all talking about here.

Another example can be with your content. Leveraging content is all about re-using content you've done once in a different way so you don't have to re-invent the wheel every time. A lot of people will refer to this as repurposing. It's a great way to really spread the word and be everywhere without having to think of brand new pieces of information every week (which can be quite time consuming).

So what are we actually talking about when we say "re-using" or "repurposing?" What we're talking about here is actually taking one piece of information – let's start off with a blog post – and re-using it or repurposing it in lots of different ways.

A great example is you've got your blog post. You might actually read that blog post out as a transcription audio file and load it up as a podcast, for example, that someone can actually listen to.

You might actually read your blog post out face-to-face to a camera and you might have some charts or some information that you may want to share. This could be turned into a YouTube video, which you'll then share with a different group of people.

You could just extract certain points and start a conversation on a forum.

You will create some Facebook posts that you could link on it.

And you can even share your blog post on LinkedIn and within conversations on LinkedIn as well.

So with one piece of information, one piece of content, you've been able to interact with lots of different groups of people in lots of different ways without having to re-invent the wheel.

Why would you repurpose or re-use your content? Well it saves you time. You don't have to re-design everything every week over and over again. And if you're stuck in selling your time for money at the moment, whilst you get out of it, for every single minute that you dedicate toward marketing, which is extremely important, you're not earning any money, which is why it's so important to save time.

In fact, it actually saves you money! You're don't have to go out there and use your time for inventing more content, which means you can dedicate more hours to actually earning more money.

You don't have to print your material up 10,000 times every time you design a new flier, because you can repurpose the ones that you've already got. And the whole point about re-leveraging content and re-using and repurposing is to get into the frame of mind of being everywhere.

If you think about those who are successful in their small business, these people can be found everywhere. We're just going to list off a group of areas where you would likely find very successful people. Facebook. Twitter. YouTube. Blogs or forums. LinkedIn and anywhere else that you might find a successful entrepreneur.

People who are successful, such as us, the Ninja Business Chicks, are usually in at least three or four of these areas. You do not have to be in all of them. We definitely think you do not have to maintain all of the areas that we have mentioned in this book. But you really have to be in at least three or four, and the reason why is that different people hang out in different areas.

So the people who you interact with on Facebook are going to be a different demographic or might be a different portion of your target market to those who are hanging out on LinkedIn. Those people who hang out on LinkedIn might not be hanging out on Twitter or YouTube.

So by ensuring that you're everywhere will enable you to get in front of a wider audience without having to do all the legwork. Because as you remember with couch marketing and social media, including LinkedIn, every time you put something up and it gets shared with various people, the network of individuals that see your updates, your content, your videos, your blog posts, your podcasts, starts to spread like wildfire.

That's the power of social media and that's why you really need to get into it if you haven't gotten into it yet.

So lets get started – follow these steps below to help you leverage yourself and your business and take it to the next level!

1. Record fifty short topics (five mins) on your iPhone, smart phone or anyway that you can record an audio file. 4.5 hours approx. of work (including some thinking time!).

2. Transcribe (OR pay a virtual support person to transcribe the files) into fifty two written files. If you do this yourself and you are a touch typist this could take up to sixteen hours. You will need to work out if sixteen hours of your time is worth doing transcription OR making sales.

    a. You now have fifty two potential podcasts AND fifty two Blog posts (ready for images) for a WHOLE year. Done, dusted.

    b. You could even get your transcriptionist to upload them into your blog all scheduled in with images ready to go live automatically without your interaction.

1. Find ten blogs that have similar target markets to you.

2. Watch the blogs and comment on their posts regularly.

3. If you find that your values align – contact the owner and offer to write some GUEST blog posts. That is you giving your time away FOR FREE to write valuable articles.

4. If the owner agrees then you can work out a plan on what and when you will write.

   a. You now have the ability to get your name out in front of lots of OTHER people who are potentially not on your list or network for FREE.

   b. You are effectively leveraging someone else's list!

1. If you are going to be doing any TALKS, WORKSHOPS, PRESENTATIONS or more make sure you record it. If you make products, even record the time when you get supplies or when you are manufacturing your product.

2. Edit the recording (even if it's only for an hour) into at least eight different forty five second snippets as tips or teasers to your products.

   a. You now have eight weeks of teaser YouTube videos ready to share over eight weeks before a product or service launch. Loading eight short videos into YouTube will set you back about an hour and a half depending on how detailed your description box, tags and more are used.

I am sure with these three examples you can see how LEVERAGING yourself and the work you do will help you increase your sales and you'll grow your following without necessary doing ten times as much work. You have re-used a video recording (of a workshop you were going to run anyway) into teaser videos AND created podcasts and blog posts at the same time.

So be creative and think before you do anything – consider how else can I use what I am about to do? Where will it benefit me later on?

If you have any questions or ideas you're more than welcome to share it with these Ninja Business Chicks at team@ ninjabusinesschicks.com.au for more ideas.

Chapter 11
Your Toolkit For Success

Now that we've gone through many different techniques that you can include in your ninja couch marketing strategy, this chapter is going to go through the tools and resources you can use to make your marketing strategy explode, to manage it, to look after it and to make it easier.

We're going to talk a little bit in the next chapter about your plan of attack. How you're actually going to manage your couch marketing strategy. The worst thing you can do is actually pick two or three of these, or all of these strategies, and then do them for a week or two weeks or one month and then not follow through.

We really want to emphasise in this book about marketing from the couch, that it is very important that you actually follow through and you keep going and you have that consistency, because the consistency is what gets those clients through the door.

Let's talk a little bit about the technology that's available to you. If you're on a Mac, as the ninja business chicks are, you will automatically have certain programs that are quite handy for doing couch marketing. This includes things like iMovie, which enables you to edit and upload videos or movies, quite easily to YouTube.

So we'll go through each of the various pieces of technology and a little bit about what they do and how you can use them, and any rough guides or associated costs. Obviously at the time of writing – you may be reading it a couple of years later and costs might change – so we're just going to give you a rough idea.

The first technology is iMovie, a Mac-related basic video editing program. It comes automatically with your MacBook Pro or your MacBook Air. It is a very easy to use video-editing tool that enables you to add little introductions or menus or the banner down at the bottom that has text. And then you can link it directly to your own YouTube account enabling you to publish the video directly to YouTube, which is fantastic. iMovie costs nothing if you own a Mac, obviously, because it comes automatically and it's very simple to use.

If you're not sure how to do something, you're more than welcome to contact the Ninja Business Chicks at team@ninjabusinesschicks.com.au or alternatively, YouTube. We're talking about YouTube here, so if you actually YouTube how to X, Y, Z in iMovie, if you Google that phrase in YouTube, chances are somebody's already recorded the video on how to do it.

Now if you're not on a Mac, there are other video-editing programs that are available such as Camtasia. Camtasia actually works on Mac and PCs and you can trial it for thirty days for free. This is fantastic particularly if you recorded a whole lot of movies and can do a lot of editing in those thirty days to get you going. If you have the capacity to record twelve or twenty four movies and you're doing one a month, you could probably edit them all in your thirty-day trial period just to get yourself started. So if you're organized, then you can really take advantage of that thirty-day trial period. If you need to use it continuously after the thirty days, which you probably will, then you would have to purchase a license for it or download it. At the time of writing it's in the vicinity of $100 for a Mac.

Another video recording tool (recording not necessarily editing) is JING. Jing will allow you to record your screen for up to five mins which is great if you are doing a lot of "how to" videos.

Other recording software (both audio and video) include QuickTime which is REALLY simple to use. These simple tools are more or less for recording rather than editing. So if you are a one take wonder then they will work wonderfully for you.

A great FREE audio editing/recording tool is GarageBand, which once again comes with your Mac. The equivalent for PCs (or even a MAC) would be Audacity which is what a lot of people use for podcast recordings.

One of our ALL TIME favorite audio recording tools is actually our iPhone! You can do it on the fly where ever you are, right when inspiration hits!

Many smartphones (and the Ninja Business Chicks use iPhones, so they're speaking from experience), have built-in voice recording programs. You can plug in your hands-free if you want to speak directly into the microphone or you can just have your phone in your lap talking, and then you can simply e-mail that audio file to yourself or you can share it.

Once complete, simply upload it to wherever you want people to be able to listen to it.

So if you want to record an audio interview with someone, then that is a fantastic way that you're able to do it. Great if you want to interview people in your industry to provide extra content for your fans and clients.

Another way you can actually record an interview is over Skype. There are audio recording programs that integrate into Skype that allow you to record both your voice and the person you're speaking to, which will enable you to create a podcast of your interview to share! These programs include Pamela & MP3 Recorder (for windows) or WireTap Studio or IMCapture (for Macs).

Your iPad and your iPhone and other tablets and smartphones will all have the capacity to integrate with social media on the go. We're talking here about Twitter, Facebook, LinkedIn, and YouTube. Everything of that nature can be accessed via your iPhone or your smartphone and also any tablet or iPad that you're using.

This is great for the concept of working from home and "couch marketing". If you do not want to be lugging around your laptop or if your laptop is actually set up on your desk on a stand and plugged into a monitor, then this is a great way that you can still interact with social media on the couch or on the fly. If you go on holidays, you can still respond to people who are commenting on your Facebook page and you can still interact with people on LinkedIn and Twitter. The technology that's available to you now is fantastic and you really need to utilise it and make the most of it.

Seeing as how we've already been talking about Facebook for a little bit, we'll continue on with other programs that are available. In the past, there were programs such as HootSuite or TweetDeck that actually enabled you to schedule Facebook posts, so you have the capacity to actually write a whole lot of Facebook updates in one go and schedule them in with a date and time. They can include images and links as well.

This is fantastic for chunking down work. The concept of chunking is quite common. A lot of you might already know about it. It's about pushing similar jobs together and doing them in big groups rather than doing five minutes here, five minutes there which is highly distracting and a disorganised way of working.

So writing Facebook posts could take thirty seconds to two minutes depending on how detailed and how much you know your topic off the top of your head and whether you need to do a bit of research. And if you have to do that every day consistently, it doesn't sound that hard, but things always get in the way. Phone calls get in the way. You get busy. You have appointments. You have meetings. And then all of the sudden a day has passed and you may have forgotten to post something that was important to you.

We believe that you should definitely take advantage of the Facebook scheduling applications that are available to you. Now, whilst this book is being written, there's the capacity to schedule Facebook posts directly in Facebook. When you're typing in your post you can hit a schedule button and you are able to actually select the date and time that you would like the post to go live, which is fantastic.

Often, Donna the purple ninja may sit down and write out thirty posts, one for each day, and they're just general posts to keep in contact with everyone, and she can schedule them in.

One of the most important things about social media and utilizing social media to grow your business and to promote yourself is that it has to be timely. So it's fantastic that you can now schedule thirty posts in a row on certain times of the day. But you need to be able to post on the fly when topics come up all the sudden. It's important that you share with your audience as soon as possible. This is why smartphones and tablets are so handy because it enables you to do that without having to go in and schedule them.

Why is this important? Well, it all goes back to positioning once again. If you're commenting on an important piece of new technology that's just come out and you're doing it three weeks later because that's when you have time to schedule your posts (because you do them once a month), then you've already missed the boat. Everybody else has already talked about it, posted about it and commented about it and shared tips and knowledge about it. The flow of communication has already happened and you're no longer the leader or authority figure.

So yes, it's fantastic to be able to actually schedule posts when you can. They're good for the quotes and images and long-standing things. If you're having any workshops or events coming up, or any other important pieces of information that are time-specific, then just schedule them during that time.

Donna has a client who owns a personal training studio and there are many trainers in her studio. She has posted up a little happy birthday message for each of her trainers on their birthday, but in advance. There are ten trainers therefore she's got ten birthdates stored in her system. So she's actually gone in and already scheduled their birthday posts so she doesn't forget. She doesn't have to remember to do it or make a task pop up later on in her diary. It's already been done. And this is fantastic for time-saving and very efficient. However when a client brings in a gift to the trainers of a healthy snack, they will take a photo then and there and share it on Facebook live as its current at that point in time.

Another great example is clients who schedule Christmas promotions during Christmas time. Or you can schedule a once a day post if you're doing a countdown for an event or product launch. Because you now have the capacity to schedule these posts in, you can do it in a far more efficient way. The tools and resources that are out there available to you make it so much easier.

Other pieces of technology that might help you out in managing your couch marketing strategies include Dropbox. Dropbox is a fantastic online storage facility where you can store a lot of your content. The reason why we include it in this particular chapter is although it isn't directly related to a specific technique – it's more of a resource to help you manage and implement your couch marketing strategies by enabling you to store lots of files which you can then access from anywhere AND giving you the ability to share files with any outsourced team members who you are utilizing to help you with your business.

So if you have a virtual assistant that's going to be scheduling all your posts for you, but you have specific content you want them to get that off, you can share those files with them within a Dropbox folder. You can store all your videos on Dropbox and you can access them from anywhere. Once again dropbox can also be accessed through your smartphone and through your iPad or a tablet. This service will also stop you from sending large emails (with large attachments) back and forth between your support team and yourself.

Besides Camtasia and Dropbox, which costs approximately $50 a year if you're not using the free version, there's actually not that many other costs associated with marketing from the couch. YouTube is free. Using iMovie is free. Using Facebook scheduler is free. And using your smartphone and your tablet obviously is free.

Just because you're sitting at home working and you want to promote yourself doesn't mean you need to spend thousands and thousands of dollars on printing 10,000 flyers that are going to get popped into the local newspaper and probably thrown away.

There are LOTS of ways that we have shared that you can start doing today to grow your business and profit from the couch.

It doesn't mean that when you're not out there doing face-to-face networking, you're not marketing. There are other strategies available to you, and that's fantastic!

Please note that what we have listed here is not the total list of tools available to you – it's just a great starting point to get you going. It's better for us to give you the basics to get started, rather than bombard you with a list of one hundred pieces of technology to confuse you. These ones listed are the ones we use all the time and find really easy to use – so you can too!

Chapter 12
Creating Your Ninja Plan of Attack!

Okay so you have been given a whole lot of options so you can market from the couch and grow your home based business.

They are mostly free and easy to start doing right now. Probably most of you will go out and start trying some of the techniques straight away and maybe you will put in a lot of effort for the first seven days … but then life will get in the way. You will be busy with your family, your job (if you are still working whilst you are transitioning) or just simply business because your business is growing.

The worst that you can do is stop and start your marketing campaigns as this will cause a very inconsistent flow of sales and therefore flow in money hitting your bank account.

No matter how busy you are with work and life you will ALWAYS need to make time and do some marketing – this is why we have loved writing this book. By giving you the strategies that you can do from home on the couch – it will be far easier as you can integrate it into your life whenever you can.

Before you start anything ensure that you have some way to collect and maintain a list of everyone you meet and their contact details. If you are about to embark on any of the strategies listed in this book to grow your business, chances are you're going to interact with a WHOLE lot more people so if you haven't got a client database set up at this point, NOW is the time to get started so you're ready straight away.

To ensure that you have the best chance of success AND to make it as easy as possible – below is an example of a spreadsheet we want you to make. This simple spreadsheet will allow you to add various tasks in the first column and give you the opportunity to mark off each day of the week when those tasks are complete. You can either check it off each week online by placing an x in the day once complete, or you can print your checklist and tick it off manually.

Choose what works best for you.

Task	Mon	Tue	Wed	Thu	Fri	Sat	Sun

To make it even EASIER we have listed below in short points, lots of different tasks that you could allocate yourself under the various techniques. **Be sure to add your own in**.

Pick two to three techniques to begin with, master them and make them habitual before you start to add in any further couch marketing strategies.

If you want to share your completed action plans with our community then you can email them in or take a photo and share on our Facebook page!

Facebook

- Update your status as least once a day on your business page and/or personal page if you are a brand in itself.
- Share a photo or image.
- Share a link to an internal page (something off your site).
- Share an external link (a page on someone else's site).
- Share a video.
- Tag pages and people whenever you can for additional exposure.
- Comment on at least three other walls and pages with a relevant comment or message.
- Respond to any wall posts or private messages you may receive.
- Follow at least three new pages per week that you feel are relevant.
- Send a friend request to EVERY single person you meet. They may or may not accept, this is okay.
- Join and interact with relevant groups.
- Acknowledge any friend requests with a private message (aka start a conversation).
- Invite new friends to like your pages.
- Include non business items to keep it human and fun (make people want to learn more about you).

LinkedIn

- Send a connect request to EVERY single person you meet. They may or may not accept, this is okay.

- Join and interact with relevant groups.

- Share any blog posts, videos articles or any important news about your business on your news feed.

- Maintain your personal profile.

- Create a company page and update regularly with your product and services.

- Acknowledge any connection requests with a private message (aka start a conversation).

- Ask a question or answer a question in a group.

Blogging & Forums

- Create a Gravatar.

- Comment on a competitor blog post daily with a relevant message including a different link to your website each time. Comment on different posts.

- Record seven, five min tips on your smart phone (in preparation for blog posts). We have written seven here so you can add them to each week's plan.

- Get your tips transcribed ready for a post on your blog.

- Find a free forum where your target market hangs out.

- Create an account.

- Update your profile page and signature.

- Participate in conversations daily.
- Answer questions and share knowledge.

YouTube

- Record seven, one min videos on your smart phone,
- Share on your FB page.
- Let your database know that you have a new video out (or the new videos out for the month if you send a monthly newsletter).
- Add links in the description box to various areas of your website.
- Add tags to your videos.
- Add a transcription of your video in the advanced settings.

Okay so that's more than enough to get you started. We want you to fill your week with lots of different tasks from two or three techniques and do them EVERY SINGLE WEEK. Be consistent and be the authority in your industry.

As always, have fun! Marketing your business from the couch should be a fun experience where you are growing your brand and following!

Bonus Chapter
Interview With a Social Media Guru

Daniel Martin – CEO at Aston Social.

Daniel Martin is a self professed computer geek. Starting off life as a network engineer and consultant for a few technology companies, he quickly moved into the sales and marketing departments of a few different software companies. Then along came social media and marketing took on a whole different meaning. It was with this new meaning came the joining of Daniel's technical knowledge with his passion for sales and marketing. Thus, Aston Social was born.

Daniel and the team at Aston Social provide digital brand strategy and social media strategy (as well as some social media management). They take a clients real world brand and help articulate that online with the best of all the tools available. This may mean developing website scopes, finding and managing development vendors, creating social media strategies integrated with core business drivers or developing social media platforms for clients and managing the posts on their pages.

We were lucky enough to interview Daniel Martin, a social media expert from Aston Social and wanted to share it with you to help you better understand how powerful correct use of social media can be. Daniel runs the company Aston Social and is all over the latest trends and the best ways to use social media and was good enough to share his vast knowledge with us.

Ninja Business Chicks: I want to know a bit of background on where your passion for social media began. What made you start your wonderful business Aston Social? What's your big 'why?'

Daniel Martin: My big 'why.' My big 'why' is, I actually started life as a computer geek. And when I say started life, I mean when I was only five years old.

I always wanted to do something between computers and business. I didn't really know what it was. I didn't really understand how social media or technology fit into business, but I just knew I wanted to do it. And even when I was twelve and thirteen, I was running many computer businesses, just selling parts or helping people out in stores and stuff like that. And I enjoyed that.

Then I got into university and studied network engineering, computer geek stuff, and went into a few different software companies. That was computers and business, right? So I thought that was right, but I still wanted to run my own business that provided technology stuff to other businesses and make the thing fit. Working for other people wasn't ticking that box.

Actually, while I was in university, I was also doing web

development for a few people, just sort of on the side, a contract here and there. I really enjoyed that. So when I was working with these other companies, I was learning skills from the technology and the sales point of view, and then I moved to a company that did digital branding. I was their sales manager. So I learned the technology side of things that I already knew combined with social media. I knew what it was; I just didn't know how it worked. And of course I could sell it. So of course I got the whole package there. It was working with those guys that I saw what you could do, and I learned that perhaps they were doing things the wrong way, I thought. So I saw an opportunity to do it myself and do it better or differently. So I did.

Ninja Business Chicks: So which social media platform do you think is best for businesses?

Daniel Martin: That's a loaded question. It depends very much on what you're doing and how your sales strategy is built.

Ninja Business Chicks: Can you give me some examples of certain businesses and what would be best? Say, coaches or accountants? What is best for them?

Daniel Martin: It depends more on the market you're going for. Typically speaking, business to consumer type businesses – so coaches, to some degree, fall into that category – those guys would probably be best suited to Facebook. But it depends on what you're coaching.

The key with Facebook is it's all about emotion. It's about what people love and enjoy. It's about social connections and friendships and all of those things. People don't go to

Facebook to work, although I do. But most people don't go to Facebook to work, right? So they want stuff that's going to engage them on an emotional level. So whatever you're doing needs to have some level of emotional connection.

Now when you're talking B-to-C businesses, most of them do. People buy because they like the brand or they like the colour of the clothing or whatever. There's something that draws them in.

On the flip side of that, if you talk about very much a B-to-B business – accounting, I think, falls into both categories. We actually have two accounting firms that are our clients. We've got them on both LinkedIn and Facebook. So it works in both instances.

But if you're pure B-to-B, so your end clients are only businesses, LinkedIn is the way to go. What you do is you use it as a sales tool. You don't worry too much about the viral marketing concept of LinkedIn. You can, but in Australia it's a longer play. In the U.S. it works well. But in Australia it's a longer play.

Basically, the idea is, you use it as a lead generation tool and you work it really hard. Get yourself looking good. Get some endorsements. Get some recommendations. And then go out and prospect, prospect, prospect, prospect. It's basically replacing the cold-call.

Ninja Business Chicks: How do you prospect? Would you inbox people?

Daniel Martin: You just add new connections. So find who you want and invite them to connect.

Ninja Business Chicks: And they'll check you out? Who you are?

Daniel Martin: Right. It's a great way of qualifying new leads without having to actually talk to people. It works well.

Ninja Business Chicks: So how do you help businesses benefit from social media?

Daniel Martin: The biggest thing, really, to start with, is understanding the businesses' 'why.'

Ninja Business Chicks: Actually, that was one of my later questions. I'll just ask that one now because I think we'll cover off that one. I've heard you talk about the 'why' about the business and to use this as the attraction strategy. Can you explain a bit more on this?

Daniel Martin: OK. I'll answer that later.

Basically, most businesses say, 'We want to get onto social media.' And we say, 'Good. Why? Why, and what for?' Then, they say, 'Oh, OK. Well, we just need to be on it because we know we need to.' Well no, that's not good enough. You need to know why your business would be bought from. So why do your customers buy from you? Then, once you understand that, then you need to figure out which social mediums best fit for you: LinkedIn, Facebook, Twitter, whatever it might be.

And then when you've got that wide find, you use that to propagate your message on those various platforms. So use Facebook as the example. What you do is easy to define. How you do it is relatively easy to define. Why you get up every day to do what you do is a hell of a lot harder to define unless you are seriously, emotionally attached to the business. People buy from people they can relate to. The product or service is just a byproduct of that. If your 'why' is very strong, and you know you can stand by that, and then you can articulate that on various social mediums, people will relate to you and they'll connect to you and they'll want to buy from you, ultimately.

That's why good salespeople are good salespeople and bad ones are bad. It depends on where you live. Are you living in the why or the what? The very first thing I usually say to people is, 'Understand the 'why.'' Then we say, 'OK, what does your target audience look like? Who's buying from you now?' So we can define there what your message should roughly look like and then what platforms you should go into.

And then we talk about things like content streams and fan acquisition strategies, both of those being the underpinnings for any of the said mediums that you're on. So the very first thing: what's the 'why?' Who are you trying to talk to? What technology are we going to use? And then what content streams and what fan acquisition strategies are you going to use at the back of that?

Ninja Business Chicks: Take me through a social media strategy you use that others can benefit from and do themselves if time allows.

Daniel Martin: Probably the LinkedIn one would be the easiest. Facebook, to be done properly, takes a lot of time and effort, particularly for businesses that don't have a personal face. So for coaches it might be a little bit different because there is a very personal face to that, and you're selling yourself. You're not selling a product or service, whereas if you're selling a product or service, your 'why' becomes really, really pivotal because you wouldn't normally think of that.

'We sell pest control.' Well, yeah, that's not emotional. Why did you get into pest control? 'We want to make money.' No, that's the wrong idea. Why do you do what you do? Understand that, then people will buy from you because they believe you have their best interests at heart. For coaches, that same 'why' message is relatively easy to articulate because you do have their best interests at heart. That's why you do what you do. You want to help people, right?

So to go back to your question, what could people do? The Facebook side of things we probably haven't even got time for, and it's very, very big. The LinkedIn one as an example, though, is a really good one, because as I said, you can use it as a person. If you are in a business, you use LinkedIn as a professional. So you might be representing a company because your name is tied to that company. But you're still acting as an individual. And what you do is simply build a profile, make sure you've got a good-looking presence, so the image is good, all the wording is correct, all your details are filled in.

Then you go out and hunt for connections. And you do that through your e-mail system, or you connect with as many people as you possibly can. Networking events, e-mail, whatever. Then you get asked for endorsements and recommendations. Then you go prospecting.

And that is as simple as what? Let's pick a general geography and a general business type. Hunt through the people. I think with you, here's my little spiel. The spiel is really important. It can't just be, 'I'd like to connect with you.' It's got to be, 'I'd like to connect with you because I believe I can add value to your business for this, this and this reason,' or something to that affect. If you're interested in hearing what I have to say,

I'd love to connect with you. Regards, Daniel.' Something like that.

Send that connection. Send heaps of those. I mean, imagine making fifty cold-calls in a day. That would be a pretty big number, right? Well on LinkedIn you can do fifty connections in half an hour. Send, bang. Send, bang. And there you go.

Ninja Business Chicks: Because some will respond.

Daniel Martin: The response is the next step. A half-hour on Monday morning, send out a whole bunch of connection requests. By Wednesday, you'll know which ones have accepted and which ones haven't.

Of the ones that have accepted you then go in and say, 'Thanks very much for accepting. I think I'm really going to add some value to your business for these reasons. I won't waste your time. If you're interested I'd like to come and spend half an hour with you. Grab a coffee. I tell you what, I won't even sit down. I'll stand up and do all the talking. I will make sure that I'm using exactly my half-hour. Would you be interested in meeting me?'

You go to the sales pitch right then. Give people the opportunity to accept you or not accept you, because they've already gone halfway in. They've answered the phone call, right? Then it's all offline.

Ninja Business Chicks: Okay. So when do you make the phone call? Once they've accepted you?

Daniel Martin: No. The phone call was a metaphor. That connection request? That's the first phone call. So imagine you make fifty phone calls. You might get twenty five of them answered.

Well, the accepting versus not accepting, that's the answering versus not answering. So if they've answered, then you've got to go back in there and say, 'Thanks very much for accepting the connection request. I'd like to catch up with you. I'll take only ten minutes of your time,' or whatever it is.

Ninja Business Chicks: Is it something you can do on Skype if it's not local?

Daniel Martin: That's a possibility as well. The key to that is people don't like their time being wasted, so in that you've got to be short and you've also got to say, 'I will only take ten, fifteen, twenty minutes.'

Ninja Business Chicks: So you give them a time limitation.

Daniel Martin: Yeah. 'I will tell you about these things. But I will only ask that you give me ten minutes of your time. If I go a second over you can hang up.' And then you've got to make sure you're on target when you do that. You've got ten minutes. You know you've got ten minutes. But you can do that. You've opened the door. You've opened a door that you didn't have before. That's cold-calling LinkedIn style.

Ninja Business Chicks: In your opinion, should everyone in business use social media?

Daniel Martin: No.

Ninja Business Chicks: No? Could you give me examples of businesses that shouldn't? Or that wouldn't benefit from it?

Daniel Martin: It depends heavily on the market that you're going for.

For example, businesses that might be having a large number

of trade-ins. If their target market isn't on social media, there's a big argument to say that you should still be there anyway, and you should. But if you haven't got the time or the money or the resource to invest and make it work properly, then don't do it at all. Because a lot of businesses out there say, 'You know what, it is a channel that we want to do. That we want to attempt. But the target market that we're looking for isn't actually on social media. But we still want it as a channel. Uh, we'll get the receptionist to do it.'

Ninja Business Chicks: So if you're going to do it half-arsed, just don't do it at all.

Daniel Martin: Because the potential for negativity off one individual is huge. And here's what would happen. You've got the receptionist looking after it. You change receptionists because that happens to me often. They've been doing Facebook. They've been Tweeting and whatever every single day and it's all wonderful.

A new receptionist comes in and she doesn't know a thing about it. You happen to get a disgruntled customer. Disgruntled customer gets on there and leaves a whole bunch of negative comments. If you're not paying attention to it, that negativity is a really big problem. If you are paying attention to it, then the negativity is a massive opportunity. But if you're not looking, you'll never know, right? So you've got to be committed. And you've got to be aware if you're not committed. Draw a line.

Social media, to be done properly, takes a lot of resources. You want to be creating new content, new ideas, and getting stuff that people actually love and want to engage with. It's not that easy.

Ninja Business Chicks: So how would you engage people?

Daniel Martin: Basically what we do is we look at the businesses' 'why' and then we build content streams off the back of that. So the content steams fall into one of three different categories: thought leadership, humanizing the brand and sales promotions. So we have three different content streams and we end up with whatever the company has in their business that fits into those categories. Often we find we get lots of thought leadership. Sometimes there's lots of humanizing the brand. It depends on the type of business that it is. We try and take the content that they already have, maybe put a spin on it, and then put that out to the marketplace.

So, for example, with Andresen McCarthy Partners, we've got this thing called Dave's Corner, which you may or may not have seen. It's still in – I mean, they're very, very new clients. It's all in its infancy at the moment, but the idea is, Dave gets this tax update once a month. And he calls out six key points from that. Simple ones. Sends it to us. So he just cuts and pastes and sends it to us. We've got an image that's got his face in it, smiling, and we put in really layman's terms what that update means. That's stuff that people actually care about. They don't necessarily understand it yet, but the idea is they care about it and then we give them just enough for them to kind of, 'Gee, really? Superannuation-managed fund, blah, blah, blah, oh, yeah. I need to know about that.' And people are interested in some of those minute things because it's important to their lives. Not just their business.

So that's a content stream that actually crosses between humanizing and thought leadership. It is predominantly thought leadership, but because we've got Dave's face in it, it's all about people relating to this guy Dave. And it's a whole new world and a few other guys have just been getting in there and liking it and having a bit of a joke about the sort of things that he's been saying. It's a slow boat. Social media doesn't happen overnight, but you keep doing a little bit of activity like that.

Ninja Business Chicks: We've just covered whether you should connect with people to grow your profile, which you said you should.

Daniel Martin: There's only one caveat on that. I am first and foremost a salesperson. So the way I approach things is if it can't be sold, there's no benefit to it. Now I don't mean that rudely. What I mean is, as a business, you need to sell to get clients. You know that as well as anyone else. If you are not willing to have a conversation with someone that you've never met, don't go out there and chase connections. Because you will look stupid.

Ninja Business Chicks: What are some of the don'ts around social media?

Daniel Martin: Don't sell yourself continually. People always get on there and say, 'We do these things good. We do these things good.' I've seen real estate agents that get on there: 'New listing. New listing. New listing. New listing.' Who gives a shit?   I can get all that on realestate.com today if I want it. Social media's not the place for that. That's a really big don't. Don't get on there and just continually sell yourself.

Ninja Business Chicks: Give us your top three don'ts.

Daniel Martin: Top three don'ts: don't go in and sell.

Don't be sporadic. So don't fill up my news feed, don't give me fifty things in half an hour, and then nothing for three days. I follow a business at the moment that does that routinely. It so happens they have car parts that I'm interested in.

Don't treat it as a joke. That's important. But I would expect that any respective business owner would not do that anymore, but if they do, that's a big one. People don't like negative people. It just doesn't work. And social media is an extension of the real world. Therefore, if you've got negative people that you're hanging around, then you'll see negative stuff on Facebook. Spin that around, if you hang around positive people, you'll always see positive stuff. That's what you want to see. You want to see the happy stuff. You don't want to see the bad stuff.

But the other thing I would say there is don't get in there expecting it to turn the world on its head straight away. Because it doesn't work that way. And don't expect to go in there and have a magic bullet either.

I sell social media to people all the time. But we at Aston Social do not work in isolation. You can't. You cannot work in isolation because I've got to say to the client, 'We need some of this and we need a bit of this. I need you to give me back this. We're integrating back into your business to get X, Y and Z.' Open those channels. I will tell you everything that I need. Give it to me and we'll make something off of it. If you don't help us out, it's never going to work.

Ninja Business Chicks: As a businessperson, I believe you also need to be established and even in the circles that you network with face-to-face to become more known.

Daniel Martin: Yeah. It's exactly the same. Social media is networking on the internet. That's all it is.

Ninja Business Chicks: What's your opinion on using your private profile for business, or should it be strictly the business fan page?

Daniel Martin: It depends on what you're doing. For the most part I would say strictly the business page, and there's one very good reason for that. But the scenario where you could use your personal profile is if you have a super-duper personal relationship with your clients, which in the case of coaching, it might be the case. Then it might be OK. But you've got to be aware that as a friend, they can see everything that you're seeing.

Now here's where it gets curly. As a friend, you can also see what they are posting. But if you use your personal profile as a business tool, you are limiting your audience. Because a friend connection is a high-value investment. So if you're thinking of dollars, if you've got a friend, it might be worth $10 for that friend connection. On a business fan page, you have fans and not friends. So the concept is different. I can like a page and become a fan and the investment is really, really small. And in actual fact, compared to that $10, it's about fifty cents. As the business owner, you don't see my stuff as a fan, so it's a one-way relationship, which lowers the risk for the fan.

So if I say, you know what, I know that Natasa's got some interesting stuff going on. I'd like to follow it, but I don't actually know her that well. I don't want her to see what I post on Facebook. Maybe I'll just like her page. And then I'll get to see what's going on, because I'm pretty sure she's got some great ideas that I want to hear, but at least I'm secure in the case that she doesn't really get to see who I am. I'm not a client of hers yet. She's not going to try to sell to me. I've just got that safe feed of info. It's that concept that makes a huge difference to whether you should have a business page or a personal page.

Ninja Business Chicks: How does a business grow their fan page to have more likes? Do you have a couple of strategies to share?

Daniel Martin: That fits into the back of the things we call fan acquisition strategies. Basically there's two sets: online and offline. Online is everything you can do online. Offline, ditto. One of the really simple ones that people tend to jump towards is Facebook advertising.

Now Facebook advertising is effective in a certain market area, but for the most part, particularly given that the cost of Facebook advertising is increasing, the return's not that great. So actually I don't tend to push people towards Facebook advertising, unless you get some credits or something which you can play around with. Yeah, sure, do it. But for the most part it will cost you money and the return won't be that great. You can do things like Facebook competitions. Facebook competitions are very good at growing a fan base at the moment because people have to "like" your page to enter the competition, so you give away something. You give away an iPhone or an iPad or whatever. Everyone's giving those away these days. All I have to do is go to the page, "like" it, and enter the competition, that's easy. I'll do that.

Short of making it a city centric scenario, they're the best-qualified "likes" that you will get. Because you can get "likes" from people that are in Uzbekistan. They're worth nothing to you. Now I don't mean that rudely. You can't sell to those people, so there's no value in them. Whereas if you have a competition that is, you get an iPod. Well I'm sorry, you've got to be in Melbourne because you've got to come pick it up. There you go. You get Melbourne people only. And you grow a Melbourne fan base.

The numbers might not go as high, but it doesn't matter. You're getting qualified people who actually could buy from you at some point in time. So from an online point of view, you've got the Facebook advertising, you've got competitions, which at the moment are big ones.

Ninja Business Chicks: Would you have the competition entry on the page?

Daniel Martin: You have to, yes. There's a big catch there. A lot of people are saying, '"Like" us to enter our competition.' It doesn't work that way. If you do that, you can have Facebook actually take down your Facebook page. It doesn't conform to their rules.

Now, people do it all the time. And I have seen people lose their Facebook page and never get it back. So you will lose it and it will go. But it's very easy – not to circumvent, but to be within the guidelines. It's really, really simple. You run a competition, and the apps that build those competitions, because we do those all the time, they simply say, '"Like" us to enable you to enter the competition. And then when they hit "like," the page changes. 'Here you go. Put your details in.' You've got your "like." So that's the way that it works.

Ninja Business Chicks: Awesome. Are there any other ways?

Daniel Martin: The offline stuff is probably the big, nice, powerful one.

Ninja Business Chicks: Where you meet people?

Daniel Martin: That's a great idea, yeah. Don't just say '"like" my page.' That's my biggest bug bear. That gets me like you wouldn't believe. We're at a restaurant last night and they had that '"like" us on Facebook' image. They'd printed it out and they had it stuck on windows and stuff. I said to my parents, 'What's wrong with that?' They're looking blankly.

'"Like" us on Facebook.' Yeah, OK. How do I get to you? I can't click on the window. How do I get to you? And then often people will say, 'Find us on Facebook.' OK, well I'm pretty sure you're called the Railway Hotel. There's a million of those. Which one's the right one?

Give people the URL. A lot of ads on TV are starting to do that now. You'll see the 'f' symbol with a slash and then the URL after it. Do that. That is pivotal. Absolutely pivotal. The page name. You absolutely need that.

Ninja Business Chicks: I thought I was saying the wrong thing for another one of my businesses but I would always say, 'Ultimate Weight Loss Coach on Facebook.'

Daniel Martin: No. Because if I type in Ultimate Weight Loss Coach…

Ninja Business Chicks: It won't come up?

Daniel Martin: It might. It might not. Facebook's search algorhythm is not like Google. Google is very open. Facebook is closed. It has what's called a search bubble. It will show you only what is relevant to you. So, Facebook.com/

UltimateWeightLossCoach. Whatever the URL is, that's what you need to give them.

That's only half the equation. So you would get up and say, '"Like" me on Facebook. My URL is blah, blah, blah.' Why? Why should I "like" you on Facebook? What's in it for me?

Ninja Business Chicks: What do we say?

Daniel Martin: What is it about what you do that interests people? So again, the 'why.' It comes back to the 'why.' I love helping people lose weight. It's what I get a massive kick out of. I'm running a Facebook page. What I'm doing is two things. I'm sharing some of the experiences of my clients, because I've got some clients that have really achieved some absolutely outstanding things, and I'm sharing those stories. And also, I'm just sharing some tips along the way. These little bits and pieces that I come up with that really help people. If you "like" me on Facebook, you'll just see those popping up. If you're interested, jump on to Facebook.com/ UltimateWeightLossCoach.

Then there's something for me to go and get. To me, that says, 'Oh, wow, really? I want to see those stories,' or 'I want to get those tips.' You're giving something away. You're probably giving that away anyway. So you need to let people know why they should.

Which is why the competition works well for people because if you're running a competition, in your own mind, suddenly you say, 'Oh, I've got something to tell people.' Because you get up and say, 'Enter my competition because I'm giving away blah, blah, blah.' You've given your spiel. But it's just a different spiel from the one that I just told you.

Ninja Business Chicks: What should people be posting on their fan pages? The tips? Mixing it up, I guess, with pictures?

Daniel Martin: So there's a combination. In terms of the content types, pictures, video and text, don't negate only text updates because at the moment Facebook is putting more weight on text-only updates. So you're more likely to get in front of your friends.

Ninja Business Chicks: Because so many people post pictures? Is that why?

Daniel Martin: They don't tell us. They just change the rules. It changes all the time. As of today, they're giving more weight to text. But it could be photos tomorrow. We don't know.

Ninja Business Chicks: Okay. That's cool. So mix it up. Is it enough to be on one platform or should we be using multiple platforms of social media?

Daniel Martin: It's enough to be on one platform if what you're doing is appropriate for that platform. For example, a lot of people say, 'I've got to get on Facebook and Twitter.' There's a really good reason why I wouldn't suggest Twitter: 11.7 million Australians are on Facebook. That's over fifty one percent of the population. Majority rules. That is steadily growing. How many are on Twitter? Do you know?

Ninja Business Chicks: I have no idea. My husband loves it.

Daniel Martin: Two-and-a-half million. And it's been 2.5 million for the most of this year. Nobody cares. And the people who are on Twitter, and that's fine. But they're there for a very specific reason. These are people's personal opinions and people's personal thoughts. Topics about current news and issues in current affairs, and people get in there sharing their personal opinions and thoughts. It's all about having this conversation with a whole bunch of people you don't know about some certain topic. That's relevant and it's interesting and all of those things. Try selling on it. It's a lot of work for not a lot of people. You're not getting to enough people in Australia. In the U.S. it is a different ballgame because there are so many more people.

If you want to do it, you've got 11.7 million people on Facebook and you've got 3.2 million on LinkedIn, you've got 2.5 million on Twitter.

Ninja Business Chicks: Do you have any recommendations on software to help you manage your social media accounts?

Daniel Martin: HootSuite's a good one. HootSuite allows you to manage all the platforms up to and including Pinterest and Google+. It's growing. It's also very, very cost-effective for those of us who play in the home game. And Sprout Social. Sprout Social is a reporting tool. It also allows you to schedule posts, but not as well as HootSuite does.

Ninja Business Chicks: Does HootSuite cost money to use?

Daniel Martin: HootSuite has a free version. I think the free version is enough for one or two pages. So probably you would cover yourself. With Sprout Social, the same applies up to, I think it's three profiles, is free. But Sprout Social is excellent. We actually use the paid version. And Sprout Social allows you to generate automatic reports that just give you demographic info, sentiment, reach, viral, organic, paid, all that sort of stuff in a really easy-to-read report. It's brilliant. It's really good.

Ninja Business Chicks: What steps should you take if someone is using your social media profile to lodge complaints? For example, do you think we should delete and deal offline or better to deal in front of everyone?

Daniel Martin: It depends on the complaint. There's a thing called house rules. House rules or page guidelines govern the way a page should be run. Basically what you're saying there is if it's offensive, defamatory or derogatory, we'll delete it. Everything else is fair game. The reason that you do that is if people go on there and start swearing, you delete it, but if people go in there and say, 'Look, I've tried to come into your store. It just hasn't worked. The queues are so long. I need some help. I'm really, really annoyed. What are you going to do?' And there could even be a little bit of swearing in there.

All you've got to do then is jump online and say, 'Really? We're so sorry. We didn't even realize that you were waiting with this issue. I'm very glad that you brought it to our attention. Now we can do something about it. If you'd like to either send me a direct e-mail or phone me on this number, I will sort it out for you personally.'

That's all you need to do. And that is more valuable than any positive comment, because the positive comments can look a bit contrived, whereas the negative ones clearly aren't contrived, and if you get in there and respond to them, it looks good. So don't delete it. Just the ones that are obviously derogatory, defamatory or offensive.

Ninja Business Chicks: How much time do you spend on social media?

Daniel Martin: Lots and lots and lots. It's often that I'll be on Facebook for the entire day. But that's what I do.

Ninja Business Chicks: Social media is largely free. What is your opinion of paid advertising such as Facebook ads? Are they a good place to invest our marketing dollars?

Daniel Martin: The paid component of social mediums is worthwhile. You just need to use it appropriately. I have seen recently a whole bunch of people saying, 'We can give you 4,800 "likes" for $500. Do you want to see how we did it?' That's a big ratio. Normally it's roughly $2 a "like" at the moment. So 4,800 to $500 is not $2 a "like." What's going on? On the Facebook advert, there will have been done by that highly, highly interesting, or they've been lying, which is entirely possible. It's been an ad that's something that attracts guys or something like that, and it's got nothing to do with the business, but it directs them to the page and it makes the page look like it's got something of whatever this thing is, and it goes viral that way. That's cheating.

Facebook ads are dwindling in their value. There's a thing called promoted posts, though, and they are the most powerful. So when you get a promoted post, what it does is allow you to ensure the post goes out to all of your fans. But it also goes out to all of your fans' friends. That's where the power is. Because it's likely that if you've got fans, there's a reasonable chance that some of their friends would also be interested in what you've got. So going out to the friends of fans is really, really, really powerful, and it costs next to nothing. You can promote a post for $5, $10, $15 and you'll get in front of 10,000 people.

Ninja Business Chicks: This is why lately they say that only fifteen percent of your "likes" will get promoted to your people, is that correct?

Daniel Martin: Similar concept. A promoted post is a way of Facebook making money off the fact of that model of your posts getting in front of everybody. It's a bit more complicated than that.

Ninja Business Chicks: But that's perhaps why they brought that in.

Daniel Martin: That's exactly why they brought that in.

Ninja Business Chicks: Cool. Anything else that you think we should know about social media that we haven't asked in these questions?

Daniel Martin: That's a big one. Don't forget the real world. Social media is not a silver bullet. It is very powerful, and done properly it can give you great rewards. But you can't use it in isolation. The most effective strategies that I've seen work have involved the real world as well. Don't forget to tell people. Give people a reason to go there. Make sure there's some bit of value. You're not looking for a trick or a hook or any of those things. It's the value that you want to give to people. And make sure that your staff or your team or the networkers that you work with – make sure they know why you want to go there. Make sure they know there's something of value there that they can share with their friends. It will all start to work, but just don't treat it in isolation. That would be the big one.

Ninja Business Chicks: Yeah, I agree with that. You've got to have a few different marketing strategies in your business aside from that, but it's a really cool tool and a free tool to use.

Awesome. Thank you so much.

Some of the key areas Daniel and the team at Aston Social help with include:

- Digital Brand Strategy
- Social Media Strategy
- Social Media Fan Acquisition
- Social Media Content Stream development
- Social Media profile posting, monitoring and reporting.

http://au.linkedin.com/danielmartinau
http://www.astonsocial.com.au

Afterword

Congratulations on getting to this point in the book. You're part of only one percent of people who purchase a book about marketing who actually get to this point. Well done.

It has been an absolute pleasure to bring you all the tips and tricks to teach you how to be a Ninja Couch Marketer. We trust that you have picked up many different tools that you will implement in your business. Marketing is not an easy skill to master, but it is fun and it can become more and more fun when you find the things that work for you.

That is why we recommend that you now go back to the beginning of the book and have a look at some of the action points and remind yourself about what we spoke about back in Chapter 1 or Chapter 4, and see what actions you can take today.

Perhaps you'd like to use this book as a twelve, thirteen-week program and focus on doing something different around your business by implementing the steps that we talk about in each of the chapters. You don't have to do it all in one hit. Break it right down. That's something that we do all of the time.

Writing this book didn't happen overnight. Writing a book

is not easy. Neither is putting together training manuals and content for different things that we like to teach people. However, when you break it right down into manageable, bite-sized chunks, then you will get it done in time.

The key, once again, is consistency. Consistency over a certain period of time and about you having the commitment to yourself and seeing things to completion.

A favorite mentor of ours, Terry Hawkins, wrote a book that is also a saying what both the Ninja Business Chicks know too well and love and that is, "There are two times in life: now and too late."

We're very open to you seeking help from us. Please feel free to e-mail team@ninjabusinesschicks.com.au if you have any questions about anything you have read in this book. We love to share and assist others to achieve the success that is out there for everyone. Come from an abundance mentality. Have a growth mindset. Invest in your education and most of all, take action.

Take action and follow through with your commitments. The only commitment that you can make is the one that you make to yourself. How committed are you? Do you want a successful business? Do you choose to have a successful business? Or do you commit to a successful business? There's a very big difference between those three.

Everyone wants to lose weight or wants a successful business however, when you say, 'I'm committed to having a successful business,' there is a difference.

Just look at marriage. Do you leave your partner at a sign of a fight? A setback? Certainly you don't, because you committed to marriage.

Look at having a successful business exactly the same. You will have setbacks. You will have frustrations. At the end of the day, if you're committed, you don't leave when these arise.

Success is not a clear-cut journey where you start from a point and you reach the tip of it. It's a mess. If you went to draw a line, right now I'd be asking you to draw a squiggly line that starts from the bottom and squiggles back and forward, all around in a circle and then ends up at the top where the arrow is pointing. That is what success looks like.

What people like it to look like is like a straight diagonal line from bottom to top. It's not that way.

Success is a journey, not a destination.

Go forth and be a Ninja at your couch marketing.

Natasa Denman's
(Red Ninja) Story

Hey everyone! I am Nat – the Red Ninja. I wanted to tell you a little bit about myself and how I got to where I am now. At the time of printing of this book, I have been in business for two years and nine months.

My journey in changing the direction of my life started two years and ten months ago. I had been employed in the Retail Sector where I managed optical outlets within OPSM and Specsavers. My husband and I had our own Specsavers franchise for eighteen months. Two years and ten months ago, my husband made a poor decision in the Specsavers business that caused the loss of that business in a mere second.

I got called out of my Specsavers store that I was managing and came home to find out the news. Initially I was relieved no one was sick or dying, but it soon dawned on me the enormity of the situation and I like anyone else went through the usual: Denial, Anger, Blame, Depression, Acceptance and Resurgence stages.

What happened was something that seemed surreal and the re-building process of our relationship and selves began. We both went to some counseling sessions separately and on my third session I made a decision I would be a life coach. I had loved human behaviour and mindset and had a Degree in Psychology and Psychophysiology, so I decided to revisit those roots and take responsibility to create my ideal life on my terms.

I had to dust myself off, stop playing the victim and move forward to achieve the grand vision I have always had for my life. So I enrolled into a $15 000 Diploma in Life Coaching at The Coaching Institute. The road ahead was exciting and filled with so many learnings and stretches. I first had to help myself before being able to help others. The first five months were exactly that. I also had an eighteen month old son Judd at home and a day job to go to three days per week while I studied every moment I got spare and networked a few times each week juggling who would look after my child.

It was full on. During the fifth month into my business I also got pregnant with my second child. I now had a pregnancy, eighteen-month old, study, a brand new business in which I worked on fifty hours per week, a day job I had to go to three days each week and then nine months in I also decided to start writing my first book The 7 Ultimate Secrets To Weight Loss.

My first business and niche was Ultimate Weight Loss – Lose the Last 10 Kilos which nowadays is a licensed 'business in a box' that life coaches, nutritionists, personal trainers, chiropractors, other health & wellness practitioners and weight loss success stories can use to add the mindset component into helping people achieve their ideal weight.

I didn't arrive at this point for almost fifteen months since starting – that is the specific branding and the business name. For the first fifteen months my business was called PRS Coaching which really didn't stand for anything. Once I re-branded, became more specific and my book came out, the flood gates opened and I filled my coaching practice very quickly.

In eleven months I finished the twenty four month Diploma, I finished the book, I finished working in my day job and had my second baby girl Mika. Finally I had some breathing room to focus on just baby, my family and business. I returned to coaching only three weeks after Mika was born as the demand was there and I had to take what came to me as I didn't want to go back to work for anyone else ever. And I never have.

I slowly realised that people were approaching me to ask how did I get to this point and how did I do it. I told them it was all around writing the book and re-branding, so I started getting hired to help business owners produce products and tighten up their systems and branding. I did this for eight months and slowly found I was doing half weight loss and half business mentoring. I formalised my second niche after two years being in business and that is called Ultimate Business Edge – Create Products For Profit.

I systemised more and more of both businesses and came to a realisation that I could only make so much seeing people one on one. I started doing many trainings and courses and webinars in both niches and got really good at being comfortable in front of an audience. I also realised that I had established myself really well and people knew who I was. Marketing myself was no longer hard, things just flowed my way. It turned out that I was being chased, not me doing the chasing as it usually is early on in business.

With the systemisation of Ultimate Weight Loss and Ultimate Business Edge, I was able to license the programs to others who would group their own abundant businesses with a fool proof step by step program with a point of difference in both. At the time of writing this book both those businesses have thirty licensees all over Australia doing amazingly well (half *have had paying clients in their first week of coming on board and a few of them have paid off their annual licensees fees in a few short weeks). I am so delighted to see coaches coach and not have to go through what I did. They also get to learn from the inside out, how all of this has come about and model that in the future of their businesses.*

Eighteen months into my business, I met Donna Brown – the Purple Ninja and we hit it off from the word go. We had a professional relationship to start off with, then decided to run a few workshops together and soon realised we had complimentary skills and that we could have fun together in business. Thus the Ninja Business Chicks was born late in 2012 and we put together a plan of launching it in 2013.

And here we are! A book written over a weekend in Healesville - Victoria, a monthly podcast 'Ninja Tips for Business Success' and an amazing online training '12 Ninja Stars To Business Explosion'. We are so passionate about helping home businesses grow and market themselves at no or low cost from the couch. That's how we did it and we know you can too.

Change is by choice not by chance!

Natasa Denman – *Red Ninja*

www.ninjabusinesschicks.com.au
www.ultimateweightloss.com.au
www.ultimatebusinessedge.com.au
email: *coach@ultimateweightloss.com.au*

Donna Brown's
(Purple Ninja) Story

Hi everyone, it's Donna here, the Work From Home Queen and I am the Purple Ninja in this duo. I just thought I would share a little bit about who I am and what I have done to get where I am today.

Seven years ago I quit my high paying job in a financial planning firm and decided to start my own mortgage broking business. It wasn't the work in particular that I disliked (I was always great in an administrative/managerial role) it was the environment and the people that I worked with that ... um shall we say ... weren't to my liking.

I had previously left a job where I LOVED my colleagues, to move into this new role so I could get new skills and a bigger salary; but ten months in and continuously saying to myself 'It'll get better, surely it'll get better' I quit. In case you hadn't realised yet – it didn't get better.

I felt sick. I had NEVER quit a job before without having something bigger and better to go to and I had a car loan and credit card to pay off.

What did I just do? It's not like me to just do something against the norm in society. I was always a hard worker, getting to work early, doing that little bit extra – but always for SOMEONE else. Never for myself.

Shortly before I quit my job I had just become a fully qualified and registered mortgage broker. It was my intention to slowly build this business and work on growing the monthly commission a broker receives every time they write a home loan for a client when a property settles. This commission lasts the life of the loan.

So if your clients have their loans for thirty years, you would get commission deposited into your bank account every month for thirty years. Get enough loans and you could slowly build a nice little monthly deposit hitting your account. Sounds like a good idea, yes? I can tell you now, VERY hard and long unpaid hours when you first start out!

It was always (and I repeat ALWAYS) my intent to get some kind of income passively OR be able to **work from home** *successfully, so when the time came for me to have children I wouldn't have to leave the entire pressure on my husband.*

Paying a mortgage is hard work combined with living expenses and although childcare was always an option; it was something that I really wanted to avoid if I could. I don't think there is anything wrong with childcare, I just wanted to make the decision that IF I could stay at home and work around my kids, I would.

I thought mortgage broking would get me there, but boy was it HARD work. Like serious hard work. I wasn't afraid of hard work, but there is hard work for a good return and then there is hard work with no great result.

Remember as a mortgage broker you only get paid when

a loan settles. So even though I could spend a whole lot of time helping a client get the best home loan, it could take them eight or nine months to find a house, then another three months to settle. Basically I often would have to wait a YEAR (that's right a WHOLE year) to get paid for the work I did twelve months earlier. That's why getting into the industry by yourself (and not part of a franchise or a chain) is really, really hard. Perseverance will pay off, but I need cash coming into my bank now! I have bills to pay you know ...

So in the interim, I thought, "hmm I have GREAT admin skills, I am sure someone would pay me to do some typing or something like that" so with some trepidation I decided that I would advertise myself as an offsite admin assistant.

It was only going to be part time and for a short while. I had a mortgage broking business to build, so I would just get some cash flow happening so I can concentrate on the other areas of my life.

At this point I hadn't even heard of the concept of a VA or Virtual Assistant – but this was the beginning of my journey down the Virtual Road!

As you can imagine, I learned a lot over the last seven years, made a lot of mistakes and as you probably guessed there came a day when I turfed the broking and stuck with being a VA, but that's another story.

Just so you know, I got my first client about four days after I made the decision to work from home doing basic admin whilst I was going to build my mortgage broking business.

Since then and as the years have gone by I have moved away from being a VA myself (my VA business still runs with my virtual team) and now I specialise in educating people in starting their own VA business from home.

Combined with mentoring and consulting I have successfully been able to carve the "Work From Home Queen" title and constantly work with various councils right up to various levels of government to help fund programs to educate people about work life balance.

Since meeting Nat a year ago, we have probably done more work together than some people do in five years of their business and it's a direct correlation to our success. So for those of you who are interested in achieving our level of success feel free to model yourself against our approach to business and our dedication to achieve our dreams.

Remember ANY action is better than no action.

Donna Brown, Purple Ninja

www.donnabrown.com.au

www.theofficebuddy.com.au

email: queen@donnabrown.com.au

Monthly Ninja Tips for Business Success

With a collective experience of ten years running our businesses from home, let these two Ninja Chicks share their wisdom with you each month, to help you explode your business out of this world!

Each month, easily downloadable, jam packed with tips and action items to help you achieve your goals.

Valued at $97, you pay just $10 per month!

Listen on your laptop, in the car or around the home – just listen and learn ... and take action.

Remember what the Purple Ninja always says – any action is better than no action!

go to
www.ninjabusinesschicks.com.au/ninja-tips

12 Ninja Stars To Business Explosion – eCourse

A self paced eCourse with lots of videos, templates and more to help you achieve the 12 Ninja Stars of Success. If you want to make this year, the year your business explodes through the stratosphere, then sign up today!

1. Future	2. Attrack	3. Impress
4. Virtual	5. Fans	6. Profit
7. Connect	8. Leverage	9. Present
10. Expert	11. Fame	12. Mindset

YOUR BONUS!

Implementation Manual

Ninja Tips for Business Success Podcast for 3 months FREE **(valued at $97)**

Ninja Couch Marketing Book **(valued at $35)**

Total Value: $5,997

You Pay **Just $797** or easy 4 monthly installments of **$199.25**!

All from the comfort of your couch!

Go to
www.ninjabusinesschicks.com.au/explode-your-business

Notes ...